ACCLAIM FOR *KEEP CLIMBING*

"Everyone seeking financial freedom should read David Rosell's book *Keep Climbing*."
—Charles R. Schwab, Jr.

"I learned so much about money and had a blast doing so. All millennials should read *Keep Climbing* so they don't get screwed. Plan hard now so you can play hard later."
—Shari Brooks, executive producer of MTV's "Ridiculousness"

"You always want to make your future bigger than your past, but that's hard to do if you haven't put a sound financial plan in place. In *Keep Climbing*, author and financial planner David Rosell shows you how to do that through his own adventure and travel stories."
—Dan Sullivan, founder of The Strategic Coach, Inc.

"A team like ours wins the Major League Soccer Championship because of great coaching and focused preparation. David Rosell provides the education and motivation needed to take you to your financial finals."
—Nat Borchers, two-time MLS Soccer champion

"Chasing financial freedom is a race we all participate in. Although it's a quad-burning, uphill battle, David Rosell's *Keep Climbing* will give you the edge as you pedal toward the finish line."
—Adam Craig, U.S. Olympic mountain biker

"*Keep Climbing* is a must-read for millennials seeking to jump-start their financial lives."
—Don Yaeger, *New York Times* best-selling author, former associate editor of *Sports Illustrated*

"We all want to be front-runners when it comes to finances, but only those of us who are motivated to do what it takes will get there. David Rosell's book will keep you climbing even when the going gets tough."
—Roger Dawson, author and Hall of Fame speaker

"We can all overcome challenges. Even though I'm legally blind, I've always wanted to compete in the Iditarod. To make that happen, I needed a good team of dogs and I had to learn a heck of a lot. If finding financial freedom sounds just as daunting to you, arm yourself with the kind of critical information contained in David Rosell's book *Keep Climbing* and you'll make it to the finish line just like I did."
—Rachael Scdoris, professional dog sled racer, author of *No End In Sight* and a 2006 *Glamour* magazine Woman of the Year

KEEP
CLIMBING

A MILLENNIAL'$ GUIDE
TO FINANCIAL PLANNING

DAVID ROSELL

Keep Climbing:
A Millennial's Guide to Financial Planning
© 2017 by David Rosell
First Edition May 2017

ISBN: 978-0-9893881-3-9

Cover design by Lieve Maas
Cover photo by Nate Wyeth

Published by
Mill City Press, Inc.
Maitland, FL

DEDICATION

I dedicate this book to my amazing children, Sophie and Jack.
I love you more than you could ever imagine. Here's to a lifetime of continued adventures.

ACKNOWLEDGEMENTS

Keep Climbing is the result of many people's time, commitment and expertise.

My sincere gratitude and appreciation goes out to those who supported me with their encouragement during this wild and interesting ride, notably ...

Mom and Dad, who always encouraged me to exploit my unique abilities and assisted me when I needed guidance over the years. Thank you for your unconditional love and support.

My grandparents. Although you are no longer with us, you each made an indelible impact on my life. **Grandma Ruth,** you inspired me to start investing into the stock market at a very early age. I probably would not be in my profession if it were not for you.

Jim Lee, Matilde Konigsberg, Susan Johnson and **Zelda** for your kindheartedness and spiritual guidance during those challenging times. You're like a backbone—always there when I need support. And **Ben Perle,** who has taught me that great friends are people who make your problems their problems, just so you don't have to go through them alone.

The entire **Tuesday crew,** an amazing group of guys who know how to suck the nectar out of life, share continual laughs and adventures, and who truly care about each other.

Brenna Hasty, my dear friend and colleague over these past five years. You have been my sounding board at work as well as in life. You live by the motto, *Do what is right, not what is easy.* Thank you for your unremitting dedication to this book, including your superb contribution to Chapter 2. You are about to discover that travel is the only thing you can buy that makes you richer. Happy trails!

Rodney Cook. I'm honored to call you a colleague as well as a friend. You're an amazingly smart man who also knows that we are in the people business more than the numbers business. Cheers to a long future together.

Linden Gross, my writing coach and editor, who has also become a dear friend. You have taught me that *sloppy copy* along with red wine eventually leads to a book I can be damn proud of. Thanks for pushing me so very hard and yet having the compassion to know when to pull back. We make one heck of a team.

Lieve Maas who mixed artistic skills with passion and designed both the cover and the book interior with love. **Elizabeth Crane,** the best copy editor I could imagine, who painstakingly reread the book many times to help ensure excellence.

Erik Janssen, a close friend and fellow financial advisor who climbed into Broken Top with **Brenna Hasty** for the cover shoot. You two millennials should be on the next REI catalog.

My fellow travel enthusiasts who know that a good friend listens to your adventures, but a great friend makes them with you. Let's never forget that there's always something wonderfully new to be found. Cheers to crazy adventures, midnight swims and rambling conversations.

CONTENTS

BA$E CAMP: NAVIGATING THROUGH THE FINANCIAL DEATH ZONE

I'd like to get a firm grasp on reality,
but someone keeps moving it.

Are you setting yourself up for financial failure—disaster, really—even though you often think about money? Are you headed for the financial death zone?

The death zone is the name mountain climbers use when referring to extreme high altitudes above 8,000 meters (26,247 feet) where oxygen is so scarce that most humans can't even breathe. At this altitude, your body begins to feel like you are about to meet your maker, as it cannot acclimate to the incredibly harsh environment. Many climbers become weak and lose the ability to think straight. They struggle with making decisions—especially under stress. Staying at this altitude for too long significantly increases the risk of fluid accumulating in the brain or lungs, a fate that has killed many. Most of the more than 250 climbers who have died on Mount Everest have died in the death zone.

Mountaineers draw on bottled oxygen to overcome the extremely thin air in the zone. Ed Viesturs is one of the few exceptions. As one of the most notable and accomplished mountaineers of all time, he's demonstrated that it's possible to stand atop the world's 14 8,000-meter peaks without the support of bottled oxygen. It is also worth mentioning that he has achieved these remarkable feats without taking the reckless chances that so many do, i.e., without succumbing to summit fever and the glory to be on top of the world.

My first book, *Failure Is Not an Option,* starts with a story:

> *Imagine that you're at Mount Everest Base Camp and you've come upon a group of mountaineers about to start their expedition to the summit. "What's your ultimate goal?" you ask them.*
>
> *How would they answer?*
>
> *If you're like most people, you'd probably assume that their ultimate goal is getting to the top.*
>
> *As you're about to find out, you'd be wrong.*

Reaching the summit is not an answer experienced climbers, including Viesturs, would ever give when asked about their ultimate goal. You see, veteran climbers know that 80 percent of climbing accidents and deaths occur on the descent. At that point, most climbers are fatigued and dehydrated. The availability of bottled oxygen and sunlight is often limited. So before these climbers even set out, they are fully aware that the second half of their journey is the riskiest and needs the most planning.

Visiting with Ed Viesturs, Bend, Oregon

Who cares? you might say to yourself. *I have no intention of climbing Mount Everest. In fact, I probably don't ever want to climb any mountain.*

Hold on. There is one mountain you're going to need to scale even if you're not an outdoor enthusiast. This ascent involves making sure you have enough money to live the life you've always imagined in the years to come. And I'm going to tell you that if you don't get it right, this endeavor could make climbing Mount Everest feel like a stroll in the park.

EVEN THE DOWNHILL NEEDS TO BE UPLIFTING

In today's world, you must successfully navigate through the financial death zone since your future retirement income needs to last the rest of your life—often more than three decades after your earning years end! This is even harder since this second half of your financial journey encompasses the greatest risk and requires the most planning. That's why in *Failure Is Not an Option,* I shared the eight risks that one faces on the financial descent and provided the financial ice axes and crampons required to overcome them.

In this day and age, however, too few will have the luxury of worrying about this risky financial descent from the top. Only 30 percent of climbers who attempt Everest ever reach its summit. Will this be a similar statistic when millennials reach retirement? Frighteningly, I believe that's certainly a possibility.

You must first make it to the summit before you can descend. When it comes to our financial lives, this means creating a well-funded retirement. Just like mountaineering, unless we adequately plan and prepare for that retirement, we will not reach the top.

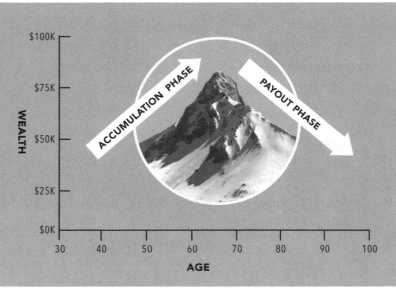

Mount Washington, Central Oregon

Every generation has had its own set of trials and adversities to conquer. However, today's generation of young adults faces a uniquely challenging environment.

In the past, if you emulated the admirable examples of your parents and grandparents as they prepared for their years of retirement, your chance of achieving success was very high. Similarly, if you followed the step-by-step advice of the many how-to books on retirement, your chances of success were also quite strong.

So far, the 21st century has turned much of the traditional wisdom regarding financial planning upside down simply because the rules of engagement have been completely rewritten. Gone are the days of pensions and defined benefit plans. Social Security has become Social Insecurity. Student loans are now the second-largest debt class, behind only mortgages. And saving for retirement is a luxury that many just can't afford.

Launching into adulthood is never an easy task, but you millennials have it pretty rough—at least compared with recent generations.

But don't give up. There's hope.

Through a combination of travel stories and prudent financial and life lessons, *Keep Climbing: A Millennial's Guide to Financial Planning* will provide you with the financial foundation that's critical to financial success. Unfortunately, I can't guarantee or even assure you that the financial coaching contained in this book will enable you to reach your lifestyle and retirement dreams in today's new-fangled world. What I *can* pledge is that if you don't learn, understand and implement the concepts within, your chances of reaching your monetary goals—or even being able to retire and cash in your fun coupons—are likely to shrink to the point where you could very well find yourself in the financial death zone.

That's why I've written this financial planning guidebook. This book will help you achieve far greater financial peace of mind, since—just like climbing a mountain—those of you who recognize and address the unique risks faced by your generation are most likely to safely and successfully meet your financial goals. So fasten your seatbelt, hold on tight and enjoy the journey we are about to embark on.

CHAPTER 1

CLIMB HIGH

*If anyone ever tells you your dreams are silly,
remember there's a millionaire
walking around who invented the pool noodle.*

I admit, I was scared. Nobody tells you how big the Himalayas really are. Actually, that's not true. They'll tell you they soar to the heavens, but until you experience them firsthand you just can't believe how colossal they are. My goal was to reach the summit of Thorong La at 5,416 meters, or nearly 18,000 feet in elevation. Although I would not be entering the death zone, let's face it, that's higher than Mont Blanc, Europe's highest mountain. What the heck was I doing here?

Yes, I had wanted to challenge myself. But did I really need to put myself through the most mentally and physically demanding trudge of my life? I guess the answer was yes.

Previous explorations had been limited to four or five days in the Southern Alps of New Zealand or overnight trips in the Rockies and Adirondacks. Compared to that, this was bona fide crazy. It felt as daunting as going head to head with Kevin O'Leary on "Shark Tank."

LEARNING THE BASICS

It took nine arduous days to reach the high base camp of Thorong Phedi at 14,924 feet. As soon as I walked into the rudimentary structure we were staying in, I noticed a sign that read:

> Richard James Allen died from altitude sickness near the top of Thorong La. 24th Feb 1991—Aged 27 Years.
> **TRAVELERS BEWARE!**

This did not do much to raise my confidence level. One obviously did not need to enter the official death zone to face demise on a mountain.

It was cold, far too cold. I could hear the wind howling. I had hoped my personal cocoon of polyester and down was going to shield me from the most frigid temperatures I have ever experienced. I could see and hear wisps of icy breath emerging from the sleeping bags of fellow climbers I had befriended from Poland, Germany and England. I was informed that waking up in the middle of the night with your heart racing at 120 beats per minute as you gasp for air is just a normal sign of acclimatization. Although I wasn't convinced I would get any shut-eye, I eventually did fall asleep for a brief period despite a feeling of excited confidence and pumping adrenaline, as well as an uneasy stomach of nerves—just like you may be feeling about your financial future.

It was a 5:30 a.m. start, well before the first rays of the sun had crested over the dramatic, rocky creations of plate tectonic forces. The stars were putting on a show for free as I switched on my Petzl headlamp and marched into the darkness, my leather Merrell hiking boots stomping across the hard-packed granular snow.

Yes, I was scared. Scared for the first time in years. My head was pounding as I fought for breath and ascended into the thin air. The more I panted to get oxygen in my lungs, the more my head shrieked. This persistent headache felt like a terrible hangover that would not respond to painkillers. I gulped at the air, feeling as though I were a swimmer barely surfacing. I felt unbalanced, not from the effects of microbrews but from the lack of air pressure. The most effective treatment is always a rapid descent, but I was determined to remain aware of my symptoms and keep climbing. Each step was labored, and those steps quickly got smaller as I concentrated on placing one foot ahead of the other. I stopped after only 30 or 40 paces to catch my breath, then mustered what seemed like my last bit of energy to continue on.

Ashley from England (sitting) and me (standing)

So much of my body's resources were preoccupied with the basic necessities of life that it was difficult to hold a conversation with the other climbers. Each of us remained in our own private world. It was just me and the mountain. Slowly, surely, I continued upward.

My Tibetan llama wool sweater with its Yin and Yang symbol, which I had purchased in Kathmandu, proved to be a good investment. Eventually the air warmed up considerably as the sun rose, painting the rocky outcrops towering above in pink and gold. I couldn't look up as much as I would have liked as the trail had become perilously steep and I was focused on my feet.

I was now being cursed by false peaks that teased us from afar, leading us to believe that the actual peak was close because nothing seemed to be higher. Every time we approached the area we thought was the summit, we were confronted with the fact that the actual peak was still nowhere in sight. In addition to the physical challenge, this expedition was also testing my emotional reserves.

By mid-afternoon, and not a minute too soon, my international group and I reached what felt like the top of the world as the mountain split away from me on all sides. I had succeeded where so many others had failed. Never before had I been this proud of myself.

I noticed colorful prayer flags flapping in the wind, strung from mounds of rocks, followed by the imposing beauty of the majestic peaks Annapurna III, Gangapurna and the Dhaulagiri range. My fellow climbers and I embraced and snapped a couple of quick pics before realizing that nightfall was approaching and our stamina was diminishing. Now we just had to get down safely. The celebration would have to wait. Sometimes—as with saving for our financial future—we must put off the good stuff for a while in order to have the opportunity to truly celebrate later.

Getting to the top of a towering mountain or financial summit takes a great deal of work. Heck, just getting started is an arduous undertaking. Before I began my Himalayan adventure, it was imperative that I have the right mindset. I had to prepare physically, learn the basics of climbing and get my head straight, just as you will need to learn investment basics and have the right mental framework to achieve your financial success.

Despite all my preparation, I was certainly humbled by my climb to the top of Thorong La. However, I was way more humbled in Nepal before the climb even started. Having my intestines surrender on the bus to Besisahar where our trek would begin was, without a doubt, my most embarrassing moment to date, but you'll have to read *Failure Is Not an Option* for the uncomfortable details. For now, just keep in mind that if you're worried about embarking on this financial journey with me, there's no way you will feel any more out of your element than that, especially since I'll be here to guide you through the monetary fundamentals.

MONEY SMARTS

Every climb, no matter how big or small, starts with a single step. In the world of finance, it starts with some core basics.

I was fortunate to learn indispensable lessons early in life before I even began climbing my own financial mountain.

I'm about to pass down a few of these very important principles to you. With this information, I am confident that you'll be equipped with the financial rope, crampons and ice axe you need to navigate your own way to the summit of your financial mountain. Your journey may seem daunting, but over time that sense of intimidation or uncertainty will transform into enthusiasm, because with knowledge comes confidence and clarity.

Are you ready for me to share some of the financial wisdom I learned early on?

There are people in one's life who act as our guides and impact our destiny. My grandma and father have been those mentors to me. To this day, I continue to pass along the financial principles they instilled in me at an early age.

I will never forget the day my Grandma Ruth changed the way I thought about money by informing me that I was now the partial owner of the country's second-largest telephone company. *How could I possibly own a portion of any company?* I thought. It was my 13th birthday, a rite of passage into my teenage years, and Grandma had handed me a gift. I opened the manila envelope to find a document titled *MCI Communications Corporation*. It looked official and even had an identification number, a corporate seal and several signatures.

Today, records of ownership are kept in electronic form, but back then, stock certificates were printed on paper. I was quite proud of my new stock certificate—proof of my ownership of 100 shares in this corporation that I'd never even heard of. My interest in the stock market peaked when I learned that everyday people could purchase shares of any public company and even have voting rights and earn profits as the company grew. I thought this was too good to be true. You will probably feel the same after you hear the rest of this story.

Coincidentally, or more likely due to Grandma's intuitive knack for the market, just months after taking ownership of my MCI shares, a jury awarded the company $1.8 billion—the largest award in U.S. history at that time. This led to the breakup of the enormous AT&T monopoly and the beginning of the competitive long-distance telephone industry. One of the immediate effects was that MCI's stock price practically doubled over night. I felt I was on the road to riches.

"Your money is working for you rather than you working for money," Grandma proudly told me. Even while I was in class at Shenendehowa Middle School or playing baseball after school with Tim Stack, a close friend since the age of 3, my money was still working for me. I had to reflect upon this notion for a moment. Once it sank in, I realized this had to be one of the most brilliant concepts ever created.

"Does anyone else know about this, Grandma?" I asked.

She informed me that many people, including my father, had found ways to leverage their time, including investing in the stock market. I was excited and intrigued.

This was just the beginning of my education about money. In fact, Grandma and Dad were about to share with me two financial lessons that would change my life and financial future forever. Few people knew these principles back then and unfortunately most still are not familiar with them today. Are you curious? Would you like to know what they are? How about a penny for Grandma and Dad's thoughts?

A PENNY SAVED IS A PENNY EARNED — BENJAMIN FRANKLIN

The next time I saw Grandma, she asked me a question that I thought was silly at the time.

"David, if you were given the choice of having a penny double every day for one month or a million dollars right now, what would you choose?"

As a young student and soon-to-be entrepreneur, it wasn't even a contest. "A million dollars for me, please!"

I quickly found out that in this case, ignorance was not bliss. Without wasting a second, Grandma shared the chart on the next page, which continues to fascinate me and to captivate my clients and audiences when I share it. I think you, too, will be astonished by the results.

South Sister, aka Charity - 10,358'   The Cascade Mountains, Bend, Oregon

DAY 1: $ .01	DAY 9: $ 2.56	DAY 17: $ 655.36	DAY 25: $ 167,772
DAY 2: $ .02	DAY 10: $ 5.12	DAY 18: $ 1,310	DAY 26: $ 335,544
DAY 3: $ .04	DAY 11: $ 10.24	DAY 19: $ 2,621	DAY 27: $ 671,088
DAY 4: $ .08	DAY 12: $ 20.48	DAY 20: $ 5,232	DAY 28: $ 1,342,177
DAY 5: $ .16	DAY 13: $ 40.96	DAY 21: $ 10,485	DAY 29: $ 2,684,354
DAY 6: $ .32	DAY 14: $ 81.92	DAY 22: $ 20,971	DAY 30: $ 5,368,709
DAY 7: $ .64	DAY 15: $ 163.84	DAY 23: $ 41,943	
DAY 8: $ 1.28	DAY 16: $ 327.68	DAY 24: $ 83,886	

As you can see, one penny becomes two pennies, which become four pennies and so on. By Day 12, I was beyond convinced that I had made the right decision, as the original penny had only accumulated to $20.48. By Day 18, I was still happy with my choice, as the penny had accumulated to only $1,310 with just 12 days to go.

What happens during those last 12 days is something that you just have to see on paper to believe. Right before my eyes I witnessed that if you take a single penny and double it every day, in just 30 days you will not only surpass $1 million, you end up with more than $5 million.

Boy, had I made the wrong choice!

Although almost everyone I have ever approached with this question thinks it will take years for a penny to reach a million dollars, a penny doubling daily is like a rocket ship taking off into space. A rocket spends 80 percent of its fuel during takeoff; once it reaches a certain point, it flies smoothly with minimal consumption.

This was my first lesson in the power of compound interest. Albert Einstein developed countless theories and principles and yet he reportedly declared:

Compound interest is the eighth wonder of the world. He who understands it, earns it; he who doesn't, pays it.

That's exactly what you're doing with those looming credit card bills and student loans. And that's exactly why we're going to help you figure out how to pay those off so you can earn compound interest rather than pay it.

So, what exactly is compound interest?

Compound interest results when interest is added to your original contribution, known as the principal. From that moment on, the interest that has been added also earns interest. This eventually forms an avalanche effect.

Because the benefits of saving early in life are so greatly magnified by compounding, getting started with saving and investing now can make a big difference in whether you're able to enjoy your life without experiencing financial worries. Start now, and hopefully one day you might even be able to live independent of the paycheck. Can you imagine working in the future because you choose to—not because you must to cover everyday living expenses?

One of the challenges beginner mountaineers often face is they're so focused on the summit that they neglect to set small goals along their journey. This lack of goal-setting makes it too easy to return to base camp when bad weather sets in or a lack of oxygen makes their head begin to pound like the morning after Bonnaroo.

Similarly, people are typically overwhelmed when contemplating the financial journey that lies ahead. But like any goal worth achieving, it's all about having the end destination in mind and starting with incremental steps. As Ed Viesturs puts it so eloquently in *No Shortcuts to the Top:*

> *Each stretch between a pair of mini-targets becomes its own private struggle. It's only by nibbling away at these immense distances that you achieve the whole.*

It may seem easier to give up on your goals and wave a red Gore-Tex jacket in frustration while surrounded by lions (you'll find that story in Chapter 3). That's what most people would do. But you're not most people, and living a life of mediocrity is just not in your cards. As Henry Ford said:

> *Some people say they can and some people say they can't. They are both right.*

CHAPTER 2

SHOW ME THE MONEY

*The problem with things that are easy to do
is that they're easy not to do.*
—Jim Rohn

Part of learning the basics—whether it comes to climbing an actual mountain or a financial mountain—involves making the right decisions even when temptation beckons.

It was January 1996—just four years after my sojourn through Nepal. Life found my backpack and me in South America traveling from Lima, the discombobulated yet enchanting capital of Peru, down toward Tierra del Fuego, the southernmost tip of the South American mainland. I would complete this overland journey by train, bus and even thumb. When it came to crossing the Atacama Desert—known as the driest place in the world, where some weather stations have never recorded any rain—I did so in an old, rented Toyota Land

Cruiser. You can probably imagine how baffled I was when it snowed that first evening. What was up with that?

Two weeks later I arrived at the quaint mountain town of Pucón, Chile, 400 miles south of Santiago. This small city of about 22,000 people is nestled on the banks of Lake Villarrica and dominated by the permanently snow-covered Villarrica volcano. Although it had last erupted in 1985, it is one of only five volcanoes worldwide known to have an active lava lake within its crater. I set my sights on looking into the caldera to see this natural extravaganza of molten earth.

Two days after my arrival, I set off to reach the 9,338-foot summit in the very early morning with a couple from Perth, Australia, whom I had met the previous day. Although the summit is nowhere near the death zone, it has its own challenges that I would have to face, including the fact that sections of the trail up this tall, symmetrical peak are especially steep. We zigzagged up the cinder cone, trying to step in the existing footprints before us.

Once on the glacier located on the top half of the volcano, I took in the incredible scenery below. In certain ways, it resembled the tropics, with aqua lakes and dense green mountains of monkey puzzle trees—the national tree of Chile—towering above in Huerquehue National Park. Because of their longevity, monkey puzzle trees are described as living fossils. I became captivated by these unique and hardy evergreens that were given their name by an observer who thought that monkeys wouldn't be able to climb the spiky branches.

We continued upward. The last hour was like climbing a vertical ice sheet. As we approached the summit, I could not tell whether the wind or spewing lava was responsible for the incredibly loud whistling sound of a jet engine revving up. I have been on a number of volcanoes around the world, but never have I experienced an active one with molten earth inside its caldera. The fumes were noxious, causing my eyes to sting. Covering my nose and mouth with a bandana, I cautiously peered over the edge at the gaping hole of glowing orange just 150 feet below. Villarrica is one of the most active volcanoes in South America, so I was grateful that the lava it spurted into the air—just like Old Faithful does with water—remained contained within the crater.

Looking into the caldera of Villarrica volcano

Fifteen years later, my friends Peter and Sue wouldn't be quite as lucky. They had decided to travel to Patagonia to celebrate the sale of the international business they had started in 1990 and stopped off in Pucón. Thankfully they were still in bed when, on Tuesday, March 3, 2015, at 3:00 a.m., Villarrica decided to awaken with a vengeance, launching lava bombs and an ash cloud more than 3,000 feet into the air. The eruption, which exceeded the height of the volcano, was accompanied by a loud explosion that roused the entire city—including Peter and Sue. "A band of cloud had wrapped itself around the peak as lava spewed into the air, giving the entire landscape an angry yet exquisite fiery orange-red glow," they shared with me. This forced the evacuation of some 3,000 people from Pucón and nearby communities.

Peter and Sue never did climb Villarrica or get to see that lake of lava inside the crater. Of course, that meant that they didn't have to make their way back down the volcano, either. I remember that part just vividly as the rest of the experience.

As I began the slow descent, I initially longed for my Dynastar MV5s—the afternoon corn snow and expansive slopes would have made for some amazing skiing as well as a rapid return. I flashed back to 1991 when I climbed and skied down Ruapehu, New Zealand's most active volcano, which last erupted in 2007. Yes, to quote a line from a popular movie in my day, "I feel the need for speed." The adrenaline junkie inside me considered sliding down on the soles of my boots, since my MV5s were at home, safely stashed in my garage. Fortunately, self-preservation prevailed. Instead of giving in to my reckless impulse, I relied on my ice axe in case self-arrest was needed, a technique in which a climber who has fallen and is sliding down a snow- or ice-covered slope stops the slide by using an ice axe to dig into the steep snow field. Having made it to the top of the volcano that day, I certainly didn't want to risk dying for a quick-lived thrill. As I like to say, failure is not an option in such situations.

Since then, I've realized just how much this all relates to finances. It's so easy to give into the temptation to spend money. Let's face it, immediate gratification can be a ton of fun. But it's a lot less fun when those short-lived rewards wind up jeopardizing your entire future—or at least the future you envision.

Consider Peter and Sue. They'll tell you that starting their consulting business—before finally reaching the financial summit and being able to retire—required financial sacrifices along the way. Some they barely noticed. Others were a little tougher. But they chose to do the right thing, even when it wasn't easy. And now they're traveling to Chile and beyond, living a life of adventure, a life they had always imagined.

You could have the life of your dreams, too, if you make the right choices now and in the future.

WHEN TEMPTATION BECKONS

It's critical to do what makes sense, even when that involves delaying gratification. It's also critical to do what makes cents—and yes, you'll definitely wind up delaying gratification here, too. A Honda Prelude would teach me that, but this lesson wouldn't occur until four years after I started my first business seal-coating driveways back in high school.

My seal-coating business involved painting asphalt driveways with a black, rubberized material that could be purchased at my local hardware store in five-gallon buckets. The purpose was to beautify as well as protect the driveway's porous surface from the damaging effects of frozen moisture that would wreak havoc on driveways during the brutal Upstate New York winters. I was never as proud as when I purchased my first vehicle—a 1972 rusted Chevy pickup—to help grow my new business.

A few years later, I was a sophomore at State University of New York's Geneseo Business School. Driveway sealing was the perfect summer business. I took great pride in the quality of my workmanship. I even offered a written guarantee that if a drop of this messy, stinky material landed anywhere but on the driveway—including the garage doors, sidewalk, lawn and even the street—the homeowner would get the job for free. Word of mouth quickly spread around my community and I had to scramble to keep up with demand. Little did I know at the time that this new business would also experience compounding growth over the years to come and eventually fund my international sojourns to

65 countries around the world when Mother Nature's freezing temperatures forced me to shut down operations for six months each year.

We all have certain days in our lives that are etched into our minds forever. Sending out a crew of employees to seal-coat six driveways in a single day without me, a first, was one of those days. I was putting into play Grandma's lesson of having money work for me rather than me having to work for money. I'll never forget the feeling of accomplishment and elation as I checked the job sites, which had been sealed to perfection without my having to set foot on a single one of them or get any black tar under my fingernails.

Yes, money was starting to work for me without me having to work for it. While my crews painted the town black, money was also working for me as MCI continued to increase in value. Life was good.

We ended up seal-coating more than 150 driveways that summer, prompting our local newspaper to run a front-page story titled "19-Year-Old Entrepreneur Seals His Success." I was making very good money, especially for a college student. Most kids would have focused on what all that cash could buy them. But thanks to my grandma, I wasn't most kids ... well, sort of.

I had admired cars since a young age. My Uncle Joe even gave me an annual subscription to *Automobile Magazine*. I thought there was nothing cooler than a 911 Porsche Targa with a whale tail protruding from the curvaceous rear. I had collected Matchboxes of this car since my youth and had posters of it all over my bedroom walls. So, it was a big deal when I decided to purchase my first rust-free new car, even if it would not be a German dream car.

When I shared with my grandmother the brochure featuring the sleek Honda Prelude I was eyeing, she decided to share with me the chart on page 40, which contributed to my becoming a true believer in the game of investing.

Grandma had introduced me to the term IRA, or Individual Retirement Account, which is an investing tool used to earmark and earn funds for retirement savings. (I'll talk a whole lot more about this and other appropriate retirement accounts in the next chapter.) She then showed me that if I made the maximum contribution at the time—$2,000 per year—into an IRA (the maximum today is $5,500 if under the age of 50 and $6,500 if older than 50) and did so between the ages of 19 and 27, and if the account compounded at 10 percent per year (the stock market average at that time), I would be a millionaire by age 65 even if I never placed any additional contributions into the account.

This impressed me almost as much as the doubling of a penny for 30 days. But what monopolized my attention was that I would have more money by investing for just eight years than if I started investing $2,000 per year at the age of 27 and did so each and every year until age 65. This is when I truly learned to appreciate why Albert Einstein considered the power of compound interest to be the eighth wonder of the world.

At this point, the difference between working for money and having money work for me was stamped into my cellular memory. I did not end up purchasing that new car. I started my IRA immediately, a decision that would forever change my life.

I began reading books on investing, creating wealth and, for reasons that are probably becoming evident, adventure travel. I must say, I was most surprised and flattered when friends and family members started approaching me with their own investment questions. I was even more astounded when I was able to answer them properly.

Looking back, it's no surprise that I eventually obtained the schooling as well as the credentials to become a financial advisor. I thought to myself, *Why not make my next career about helping others in a field of endeavor that I have become so passionate about?* Today I get tremendous satisfaction in helping my clients achieve financial peace of mind and retire successfully.

THE TIME VALUE OF MONEY

BRENNA INVESTING AT AGE 19			RODNEY INVESTING AT AGE 27		
AGE	INVESTMENTS	TOTAL VALUES	AGE	INVESTMENTS	TOTAL VALUES
19	$ 2,000	2,200	19	$ 0	0
20	2,000	4,620	20	0	0
21	2,000	7,282	21	0	0
22	2,000	10,210	22	0	0
23	2,000	13,431	23	0	0
24	2,000	16,974	24	0	0
25	2,000	20,871	25	0	0
26	2,000	25,158	26	0	0
27	0	27,674	27	2,000	2,200
28	0	30,442	28	2,000	4,620
29	0	33,486	29	2,000	7,282
30	0	36,834	30	2,000	10.210
31	0	40,518	31	2,000	13,431
32	0	44,570	32	2,000	16,974
33	0	48,027	33	2,000	20,871
34	0	53,929	34	2,000	25,158
35	0	59,322	35	2,000	29,874
36	0	65,256	36	2,000	35,072
37	0	71,780	37	2,000	40,768
38	0	78,958	38	2,000	47,045
39	0	86,854	39	2,000	53,949
40	0	95,540	40	2,000	61,544
41	0	105,094	41	2,000	69,899
42	0	115,603	42	2,000	79,089
43	0	127,163	43	2,000	89,198
44	0	130,880	44	2,000	100,318
45	0	153,868	45	2,000	112,550
46	0	169,255	46	2,000	126,005
47	0	188,180	47	2,000	140,805
48	0	204,798	48	2,000	157,086
49	0	226,278	49	2,000	174,094
50	0	247,806	50	2,000	194,694
51	0	272,586	51	2,000	216,363
52	0	299,845	52	2,000	240,199
53	0	329,830	53	2,000	266,419
54	0	362,813	54	2,000	295,261
55	0	399,094	55	2,000	326,988
56	0	439,003	56	2,000	361,886
57	0	482,904	57	2,000	400,275
58	0	531,194	58	2,000	442,503
59	0	548,314	59	2,000	488,953
60	0	642,745	60	2,000	540,048
61	0	707,020	61	2,000	596,253
62	0	777,722	62	2,000	658,078
63	0	855,494	63	2,000	726,086
64	0	941,043	64	2,000	800,895
65	0	1,035,148	65	2,000	883,185

WAYS TO BUILD $ 1,000,000 BY AGE 65 (10% HYPOTHETICAL GROWTH RATE)

AGE	DAILY SAVINGS	YEARLY SAVINGS
20	$ 4,00	$ 1,440
30	$ 11,00	$ 3,960
40	$ 30,00	$ 10,800
50	$ 95,00	$ 34,200

I have had a similar reaction to seeing Brenna Hasty, who I had the good fortune to hire as the director of operations for my financial firm in 2012, keep climbing both personally and professionally. Over the last four years she has come into her own as a licensed financial advisor, as a dedicated athlete and as a self-confident, poised individual.

This is a bittersweet time, as Brenna has decided to leave the practice and travel the world. Has this adventure been inspired by my stories in this book and the last? I'm guessing they helped her catch the travel bug. I respect her for venturing forth and following her dream.

Pushing her limits is not new to Brenna. She's done that for the last several years an ultramarathon runner. I can't imagine running a typical 26.2-mile standard marathon. I see it as a miserable and surefire way to become impaired. But she goes for it. Mia Hamm's quote could have been written about Brenna:

> My coach said I run like a girl. I said if he ran a little faster he could too.

In April 2016, Brenna completed the Lake Sonoma 50-mile ultramarathon—a rollercoaster of a race that boasts 10,500 feet of elevation gain and loss. No, thank you! But here's the deal. Even if, like me, the idea of an ultramarathon makes you want to instantly sit on the couch, I have news for you. Whether we like it or not, you and I are running a financial ultramarathon as we speak. I asked Brenna to explain this from her unique athlete-meets-financial-advisor perspective.

Brenna's Take:

I often hear my friends talking about money. Once I became a financial advisor, they would ask me how much they should be contributing to their retirement accounts and the difference between an IRA, a Roth IRA and a 401(k). Years later, many of them are still confused and asking additional investment-related questions. I have found that lots of people in my generation of millennials just haven't begun to plan for their retirement. Even fewer of them have taken that first step of saving a portion of their income. Retiring successfully doesn't simply happen. Just like in an ultramarathon, you won't reach the finish line without the right plan of action. Both start with an active decision to jump in, followed by diligent preparation.

"I don't like getting dirt and debris in my socks while running," I told a fellow runner years ago, when he suggested I try trail running instead of road running. Despite my objections, I decided to give it a shot, and before long I became passionate about my newfound sport. But that didn't mean that I could turn around and run an ultramarathon. I had to train. In the winter when it was freezing and dark, it took all the willpower I could muster to get up and drive the 40 minutes to Smith Rock to train on the hills there. On summer afternoons after work, I was often tempted to skip a run in favor of paddleboarding the

Deschutes River followed by a stop at a local brewery. But I stayed focused. I knew that on race day I would not regret the hard training.

I can vividly remember the nerves and self-doubt I felt right before my very first 50-mile race. What if I hadn't trained correctly? Would I be able to complete the daunting 50 miles? I knew I needed to stay focused and not let the what-ifs become a paralyzing distraction. And it worked.

Four months later I tackled my second 50-mile race–the Lake Sonoma 50 in beautiful Sonoma County, California. This time I felt excited. I knew my diligent training over the previous few months had prepared me as best as it could for this hilly course and I was ready to take on the challenge. When race day finally arrived, I went through my pre-race routine, trying to ignore the butterflies churning in my stomach. Before I knew it, I was at the starting line and the race director yelled, "GO!" My nerves melted away and my training took over.

Early in the race as runners began to spread out on the course, I settled into a comfortable pace. I was feeling confident–it was going to be a great day! I felt strong over the first 42 miles of the race as I experienced the normal highs and lows that come with ultrarunning.

With only eight miles remaining, as I was prematurely celebrating my finish, I hit the wall. Almost as if a switch had been flipped, I became dizzy, nauseated and couldn't move faster than a slow walk. With all my will power, I kept pushing along, just trying to reach the last aid station to get some calories in me so I could finish. My mental state was at its lowest ever in a race and I questioned if I could go on.

After what felt like an eternity, I arrived at the final aid station where I began to refuel. As I dejectedly left the aid station, I was finally able to start jogging, although slowly. As I got closer to the finish, my mental state climbed higher and higher and my legs moved faster and faster. "Just keep going," I repeated to myself. The last three miles dragged on forever, but I felt nothing but elation as I finally crossed the finish line.

Running and investing are emotional rollercoasters; acceptance and perseverance are key to survival. Just as training is one of the necessary components to running an ultramarathon, putting away money every paycheck is a necessary element if you plan on being independent of a paycheck one day. Many people do not take advantage of their employer-sponsored plans. They reason that they still have many years left until retirement and do not need to worry about saving money yet, essentially kicking the can down the road. While it is true that we still have many working years ahead in which to save, many do not truly understand how expensive it will be to live for 30 or 40 years in our golden years without a salary. Furthermore, we may be the first generation that will not have Social Security to fall back on, making it even more imperative to begin saving now.

But that's just the beginning. Ultramarathon runners know that no matter how confident and good you feel as you set out, you need to fuel correctly or your chances of finishing are greatly diminished. To maintain a somewhat steady state throughout the course, fueling early and often with electrolyte gels and aid station snacks is an imperative component.

On the financial front, compound interest is the electrolyte gel that fuels your future retirement over an extended period of time. Compound interest is the interest calculated not only on the initial principal, but also on the previously earned interest. Simply put, compounding causes a snowball effect and grows at an increasing rate every year. So the sooner you can begin saving for retirement, the better off you will be as you approach the finish line of your earning years.

Of course, all the training and fueling in the world won't help if you don't stay the course. I have to agree with the experts that ultrarunning is 10 percent physical and 90 percent mental. Over the many hours and many miles, it's easy for mental strength to wane and to allow thoughts of quitting to creep in. To combat this, practicing visualization and mindfulness helps to boost my mental game, which keeps me moving forward, even at my very lowest points.

Saving for your future isn't a sprint, it's a long, slow ultramarathon that demands determination. For some people, investing their hard-earned money in the stock market can trigger the kind of emotional response you get when running an ultramarathon. They feel euphoria at market highs and defeat at market lows. Yet history shows that 70 percent of the time the markets are up and 30 percent they are down. The ability to ride out the highs and lows and stay focused on the end goal are often the determining factors when it comes to how old you'll be before you can retire.

My generation has decades before retirement and we will encounter many down markets during that time. Making proactive decisions to fund your financial future each and every month can conjure up the same feelings of pride and sense of accomplishment that finishing an ultramarathon does, just without all the chafing and rumbling stomachs. But you just may need some assistance along the way. I sought out the right help from a coach to guide me and help me accomplish my goal of running ultramarathons. I urge people of my generation to seek guidance as they prepare for and run their financial ultramarathon, so that they can one day reach the finish line of financial independence and live out their retirement years with true peace of mind.

Brenna Hasty running the Sonoma 50-mile ultramarathon

Brenna is living proof that if you learn the basics principles, do ordinary things extraordinarily well and *keep climbing* even when the going gets tough, you will experience results that surpass your dreams. Like Brenna, I believe we all can achieve what we set our minds to. However, as you're about to see, having the right tools at hand can be downright critical.

CHAPTER 3

HAVING THE RIGHT TOOLS

Not all those who wander are lost.
—*J.R.R. Tolkien,* The Fellowship of the Ring

Coming from a small town in Upstate New York, my entire world opened up when I spent the second semester of my junior year of college traveling through Europe by Eurorail. I was astonished to enter buildings many times older than the United States' two-and-a-half-century history. I would cross borders into countries that were similar in size to the adjacent states back home, and discover different languages, currencies and cultures. As a 20-year-old, I found this thrilling.

My first taste of travel expanded my sense of possibilities and I knew I just had to see as much of the globe in this lifetime as possible. I had caught that infectious condition called the travel bug. So after graduating from college, I continued working my driveway-sealing business and then traveled in the off-season. Since I could only work during the months where the temperatures climbed to the mid-50s and above, that meant that the world was mine to savor for six months out of each year. There were so many people to meet, sights to see, flavors to ingest. I decided to spend a month in every country I possibly could. I would have never thought then that by 2015 I would set foot in Cuba, my 66th country, a year to the day before President Obama visited this beautiful island. More about that later.

I started my month-long travel stints in trouble-free countries where English was the language of choice and the United States government was not an adversary—places like Australia, New Zealand and Fiji. By my second winter, I had built up enough courage to visit more adventurous places, such as Southeast Asia. I even went to Vietnam before travel there was legal for Americans.

After four years and more than two dozen countries, I finally felt I had enough solo world traveler experience—and enough guts, or so I hoped—to spend six months meandering down the world's largest continent by thumb, bus and train. My journey through Africa would take me from Nairobi, Kenya, to the Cape of Good Hope, the southern tip of Africa where the Atlantic and Indian Oceans meet. This was not going to be an ordinary journey, to say the least.

I felt an unsettled nervous tension as Air France flight 456 from Paris set down on the tarmac at Jomo Kenyatta International Airport in Nairobi, Kenya. Machine-gun-toting soldiers greeted me with late-night stares. I was one of only a few Mzungus in sight.

Mzungu is a common expression dating back to the 18th century, when Europeans began to explore the continent; it translates to "someone who roams around aimlessly." Today it refers in a non-derogatory way to someone with white skin.

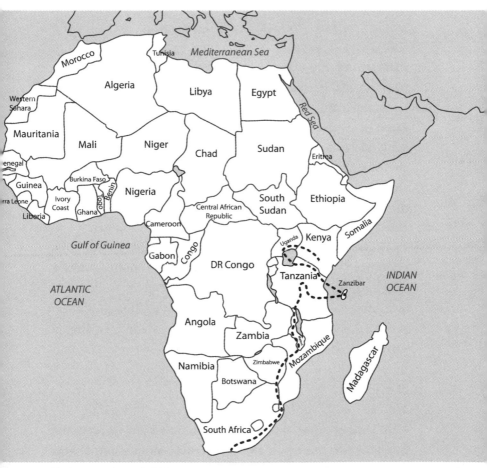

My journey through Africa

I inhaled with deep relief as I was reunited with my backpack after plucking it off the airport conveyer belt.

Now what? I thought. With four winters of travel under my belt, I had started to have the confidence of a seasoned traveller. However, landing in a third-world capital city at night and for the first time always got my full attention.

It didn't take long to meet Claudio, a pleasant Spaniard who also had just become reacquainted with his luggage and was looking for a place to spend the night. We shared a late-night taxi to the Dalat Hotel. At 420 shillings ($12USD) for the night, the hotel was one of the more expensive budget hotels listed in my *Lonely Planet* guide book, but it provided me with a relatively clean room as well as a flush toilet and sink. Even so, I placed Ziploc bags on my feet before entering the shower. Oh, how my sensitivity toward hygiene would alter over the ensuing months.

The next morning was all about a solo walking tour. Like most third-world capitals, Nairobi was congested and filthy. What a dichotomy to see shanty apartments—inhabited by underprivileged people facing a lack of reliable sanitation services, supply of clean water, reliable electricity, timely law enforcement and other basic services—located around the corner from chic hotels and contemporary buildings of commerce.

On the other hand, Nairobi, which means *place of cool water*, is as friendly as it is challenged. I was often greeted with life-size smiles, as locals were happy to offer directions in their perfect English, thanks to the British Empire's colonization of Kenya in 1920. I quickly learned that a friendly *Jambo!* (hello) goes a long way.

As I continued my leisurely walk, I was greeted by food vendors, workers, students, prostitutes, homeless people, security guards and the all-pervading safari salesmen. I already knew that a couple of days in the city would be plenty of time, so I immediately started my search for a safari company that would take me into the legendary Masai Mara National Reserve, named in honor of the Masai people who inhabit the area. (Like so many great runners, Eliud Kipchoge, the 2016 gold medal Olympic marathon runner, is of Masai heritage.)

The Masai Mara National Reserve is globally famous for its big-five game inhabitants, including the African lion, elephant, leopard, buffalo and rhinoceros. This is also the region where the wildebeest, arguably the world's strangest-looking creature, migrates to and from the Serengeti every year in what's known as the Great Migration. You may be familiar with this annual spectacle from various documentaries and from the "Lion King" movie.

There were so many safari companies to choose from, each basically offering the same service. *Where do I even start?* I wondered. I ended up choosing Game Trackers as they had been in business since 1981. My money belt benefited from booking this safari last minute rather than doing so in advance from the States. Just $370 and 12 hours later, I was on a rugged four-wheel-drive machine that could have been in a Mad Max movie or in a Red Bull-sponsored African Monster Truck competition.

After meeting the folks on board, I knew I had made the right decision. David and Kim were a witty and entertaining couple from London. Jonathan was on his first overseas jaunt from Toronto and Rebecca was his soon-to-be-girlfriend from Buffalo, NY. And then there were Knox and Toetsu, a gentle couple from Tokyo who tried their best to overcome the language barrier and understand David's British humor or lack thereof.

This was not an extravagant Abercrombie & Kent tour. Our shelters consisted of bulky canvas tents with cots and blankets that were getting on in age. No 800 thread count sheets for us. I knew, in fact, that I was truly camping in the middle of Mara surrounded by big game animals when I saw Masai tribesmen guarding our encampment with rifles. They accompanied us whenever nature called at night.

It was early to rise the next morning for what would turn out to be a very productive tour during which we encountered almost every game animal that you can think of. That included a display of two female lions devouring their recent kill of a wildebeest—unpleasant to watch yet beautiful to experience.

I was lazy and lethargic after a big lunch at camp and almost five hours of reading and writing that afternoon, followed by an unplanned catnap. I contemplated staying behind when it came time for the early evening tour before dinner, but decided to join the group of eight as I knew the experience of a night game drive is one that just should not be missed.

Steady afternoon rains from the early November skies had softened the ground. Despite seeing other companies' vehicles getting stuck deep in the mud, we had great confidence in our guide Patrick as well as our larger and more rugged vehicle equipped with chained-up tires.

Trying to push our safari vehicle out of the mud

An hour into the drive, down a grassy slope Patrick spotted a couple of lions that could not have cared less that another motorized vehicle was heading their way. Just then our tires started spinning in the wet meadow. No one volunteered to get out to place something underneath the wheels, perhaps due to the proximity of those large pussycats, so our driver continued to press down on the accelerator. It only took a moment for the rear tires to sink two feet down and our axel to bottom out. *This is not happening,* I thought.

Atop the safari vehicle, trying to get the attention of others in the distance

The sun was setting. Another band of dark clouds was heading our way. Two hungry lions that suddenly seemed too close for comfort watched us in amusement. We were going nowhere fast. As our new reality started to settle in,

I climbed out the window and onto the roof. I could make out a few authentic Land Rovers in the distance heading back to their lodge for the night. I vigorously waved a red Gore-Tex shell in the hope that they would spot us. No such luck.

As it turns out, it doesn't hurt to be able to call someone when you go on safari. These days, someone would just whip out a cellphone and dial 911. In those days, no one had even thought to bring along a radio.

"Do we have flares?" one of the other passengers asked.

Nope. No flares either.

We were unable to notify anyone. To make matters worse, we didn't even have gear to get the tires out of the mud.

This was probably not the first time this had ever happened. We took a quick inventory. No food. No flares. No blankets. Just seven sticks of Trident gum, a single airplane-sized miniature bottle of Grappa brandy and one deck of playing cards to share among eight people representing five countries. Thoughts of pizza and beer did not help. It was going to be a long night.

I always try and look at the bright side of things. I experienced the spectacular nocturnal theater as the sounds were reduced to the occasional calls and roars of the predators. Even the most frequently seen animals took on another appearance in the light of the moon and stars that sparkled in the velvety blue darkness of the Masai Mara.

We laughed in hysterical disbelief as we played with our 52 friends of diamonds, hearts, clubs and spades, and tried not to worry about the animals we could see and all the others we couldn't. We were less amused when we tried to sleep, managing only a handful of contorted 20-minute dozes. After what seemed like forever, the sun rose above the expansive horizon and help eventually arrived.

At least it hadn't been my screw-up this time. Our guide Patrick hadn't equipped the truck with the needed and indispensable gear. Once again, I had been reminded of how important it is to have the right tools at the right time. Whether you're mountain climbing or making a quesadilla, you need basic equipment to get the job done.

It's no different when it comes to investing. You must have the basic tools to not only help you get to the top of whatever monetary mountain you're climbing, but to help you survive the economic and financial setbacks that inevitably happen along the way. Just as in life, with finances you're not always guaranteed clear skies and dry veldt to drive on. So it helps to understand the terrain and have the right gear. I'll warn you right now. The material in the rest of this chapter will probably seem as big and daunting as the continent of Africa seemed to me before I started my travels there. Just remember that knowing how to select the right tools can spare you many a fearful, predator-filled night, so don't give up.

INVESTING IN THE RIGHT EQUIPMENT

Things can get confusing fast when you begin to consider the different types of retirement accounts and the different investments you can place in such accounts. I often hear questions such as, *What's the difference between an IRA and a mutual fund?* To help shed some light on the matter, I explain it as the difference between the home you live in and the furniture you choose to you place inside it.

If you are looking to purchase a new home, you have different styles to choose from. Do you like modern? Contemporary? Traditional? Craftsman? Some homes are more energy efficient than others and they certainly have different costs associated with them.

Investment homes are the accounts such as IRAs, Roth IRAs, 401(k)s and 403(b)s, among others. They are tax-advantaged accounts intended to supplement income after retirement. Similar to the homes you live in, each of these investment homes has different styles, benefits, costs and pros and cons, all of which are regulated by the IRS.

The furniture inside of these homes is the actual investments, including individual stocks, bonds, mutual funds, ETFs (exchange-traded funds) and even precious metals, to name a few.

For better or worse, retirement accounts and the investments you may place inside them don't come as one-size-fits-all. Let's take a more detailed look at the investment tools—both the prudent investment homes (accounts) and the viable furniture options (investments) to place inside of these homes—that could make a big difference for your financial future. This information may save you from having to share a miniature bottle of Grappa with your friends in your years of retirement.

HOME SWEET HOME

Many employers offer their employees the ability to defer a portion of their paycheck into retirement accounts. Examples include 401(k)s for profit businesses and 403(b)s for nonprofit enterprises. If your employer does not offer such a plan or you're self-employed, you may set up an individual plan called an IRA or Individual Retirement Account, which is simply a tax-advantaged account that can hold your retirement investments. Either way, the money you invest in these accounts will not only help you save money, it will save you taxes either now or later on.

Unfortunately, a lot of people seem to be intimidated when it comes to getting started on this front. But I think you'll be surprised at how simple it is to set up such an account and begin contributing to it.

As the type of retirement account you choose can significantly affect your long-term savings, it's worth understanding the differences between them in order to select the one that's most appropriate for you. The two most common types are regular IRAs (also known as traditional IRAs) and Roth IRAs. Let's compare them.

ADVANTAGES OF THE TRADITIONAL IRA
1. Tax savings now
2. Tax-deferred growth
3. Compounded growth

1. Tax Savings Now
Annual contributions to traditional IRAs are made with pretax dollars. This means that you are lowering your adjusted gross income (AGI) as well as your tax burden each year you make a contribution. For example, if you were to earn $50,000 this year and you decided to contribute the maximum $5,500 into an IRA, your AGI would decrease to $44,500 and you would then be taxed on this lower amount, saving you money now.

2. Tax-Deferred Growth

Whether you're a millennial or a baby boomer, taxes can take a significant bite out of your savings. This is where IRAs come to the rescue as the earnings inside of an IRA grow tax-deferred. This means your investment earnings such as interest, dividends and capital gains accumulate free of any taxes until you take withdrawals in retirement. Keep in mind that eventually you'll have to pay the taxes you've deferred on your retirement savings. But here's the good news—you'll probably find yourself in a lower tax bracket during your retirement, so the taxes you pay may be less than if you had paid them during your working years. Tax deferral also allows the portion of earnings that would face taxation outside of an IRA to benefit from the magic of compound growth. More money for you and less for Uncle Sam. Sounds pretty good, eh?

As a picture says a thousand words, let's view the power of tax deferral in the chart below. It illustrates a hypothetical $10,000 investment that experiences a conservative 6 percent annual return over a 30-year period. It also demonstrates three different tax scenarios:

- ✓ An investor who experiences tax deferral
- ✓ An investor in the 20 percent tax bracket
- ✓ An investor in the 40 percent tax bracket

3. Compounded Growth

The tax-deferred account grows to over $57,000. This figure is almost twice as much compared to the same investment growing in a taxable account while being in the 40 percent tax bracket! The benefits of tax deferral and compound growth inside of an IRA can make small, regular contributions grow into more than you might think. Remember that penny-doubling chart Grandma Ruth showed me?

Keep in mind that you can't access the funds inside your IRA without penalties until you turn 59½. That's the bad news. However, the good news is that you can't access the funds inside your IRA without penalties until you turn 59½.

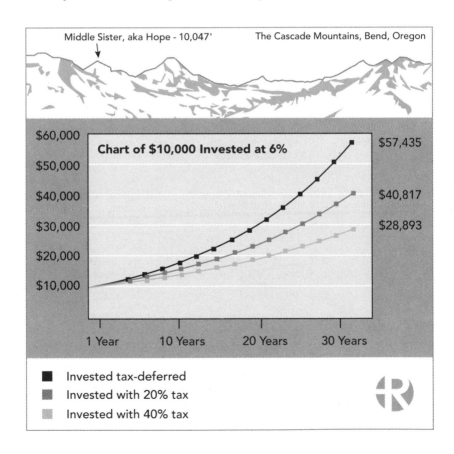

Middle Sister, aka Hope - 10,047'   The Cascade Mountains, Bend, Oregon

Chart of $10,000 Invested at 6%

- ■ Invested tax-deferred
- ■ Invested with 20% tax
- ■ Invested with 40% tax

	Traditional IRA	Roth IRA
2017 Contribution Limits	$5,500/year. If you're age 50 or older, it increases to $6,500/year.	$5,500/year. If you're age 50 or older, it increases to $6,500/year.
2017 Income Limits	Anyone with earned income can contribute, but tax deductibility is based on income limits and participation in an employer plan.	Single tax filers with modified AGIs of less than $133,000 are eligible to fund a Roth IRA. (The amount you can fund begins to decrease when your income reaches $118,000.) For married couples filing jointly with modified AGIs, those numbers are a maximum of $196,000 to fund, with the decrease starting at $186,000.
Tax Treatment	The tax deduction happens in the contribution year. Ordinary income taxes are owed when withdrawals are taken.	There are no tax breaks for contributions. Earnings and withdrawals are tax-free in retirement.
Withdrawal Rules	Withdrawals are penalty free beginning at age 59½. Required minimum distributions must begin at age 70½. Beneficiaries pay taxes on inherited IRAs.	Contributions can be withdrawn at any time in a tax-free and penalty-free format. After five years and age 59½, all withdrawals are also tax-free. No withdrawals are required during the account holder's lifetime. Beneficiaries can stretch distributions over many years and will owe no tax.
Additional Benefits	Contributions lower the taxpayer's AGI, potentially qualifying them for other tax incentives. Up to $10,000 in penalty-free withdrawals is allowed to cover first-time homebuyer expenses, but taxes are due on the distributions.	After five years, up to $10,000 of earnings can be withdrawn without penalty to cover first-time homebuyer expenses.

ADVANTAGES OF THE ROTH IRA

Roth IRAs are similar to traditional IRAs in that they have the same funding limits. Yet they have several significant distinctions, including how they're taxed. While both traditional and Roth IRAs provide generous tax breaks, the timing of when you get to partake in them is different.

Let's compare the differences between these accounts side by side:

As I shared above, traditional IRA contributions are made with pre-tax dollars and you are required to pay income tax when you take withdrawals at retirement. Roth IRAs are funded with after-tax dollars, which means you pay taxes on money going into your account so your distributions in retirement are 100 percent tax-free. Because every dollar you stash inside a Roth IRA is your money—not a tax-subsidized gift from Uncle Sam—you can access your contributions (but not any investment gains you may experience) any time tax-free and penalty free.

Should you choose a Roth IRA? If you expect that your income, and therefore your tax rate, will be lower when you retire, a traditional IRA that helps reduce your taxes now might make more sense than a Roth IRA. On the other hand, given today's historically low federal tax rates and the hefty U.S. deficit, many economists believe that federal income tax rates will rise in the future, meaning Roth IRAs in which you pay the taxes now rather than later may be the better long-term choice. In fact, Roth IRAs are ideal savings vehicles for young, lower-income millennials who may not miss the upfront tax deduction and who will benefit from decades of tax-free, compounded growth. Roth IRAs also appeal to anyone who wants to minimize their tax bite in retirement.

Another distinction between traditional and Roth IRAs is when withdrawals must begin. With a traditional IRA, you'll typically have to make annual required minimum distributions (RMDs) once you turn 70½. A Roth IRA allows you to control when you make—or don't make—withdrawals. Since a Roth IRA doesn't require any withdrawals over your lifetime, your Roth IRA can continue to grow tax-free if you do not need the funds.

Smart young savers invest in IRAs. However, really smart young savers know to save in a Roth IRA as well as their companies' 401(k).

401(k)s

Unlike the days of your parents and grandparents, most people in the workforce today can no longer depend on receiving a pension when they retire. Unless you're employed by a government agency, are a teacher or have a union job, pensions are on their way to extinction. Back in the day, a majority of employers offered pension funds that paid out a steady income over the course of an employee's retirement. But as the cost of running these guaranteed retirement income streams escalated, employers started replacing them with 401(k)s, which have become the most common type of retirement plan available today.

So, you've always heard of 401(k)s, but what are they? How do they work? Should you be part of such a plan? Let's take a look.

A 401(k) is a retirement savings plan offered to you through your employer. It's named for the section of the tax code that governs it. Here's how a 401(k) works:

💰 You decide what percentage of your salary you would like to contribute each year up to the maximum pre-tax limit of $18,000. If you're 50 or older, you may make a catch-up contribution of an additional $6,000, for a total of $24,000. Your employer deposits the money into your individual account on your behalf through a payroll deduction. These funds come straight out of your paycheck and directly into your account automatically, without you having to lift a finger. It doesn't get an easier than this!

💰 Although employers serve as the plan sponsor for the 401(k), they don't have anything to do with investing your contributions. Employers hire another company such as a brokerage firm or mutual fund company to administer the plan and the investments, but you remain in charge of deciding how you would like to be invested among the numerous investment options available in your plan. Most plans offer a combination of stock, bond and money market investments, and if you work for a publicly traded company, some plans even offer shares of your employer's stock. Chapter 7 will help you become skilled on how best to balance the various sectors of the financial markets and why you don't want to own too much of your company's stock.

So why should you take part in such a plan if it is available to you?

💰 It enables you to invest a portion of your paycheck before taxes are taken out. Yes, your paycheck will be smaller as a result of planning for your future; however, thanks to the tax benefits, the financial hit may not be as much as you might think. If you earn $50,000 and fund your 401(k) with $10,000, your taxable income shrinks to $40,000, which will save you significant taxes you would have otherwise paid. As with a traditional IRA, you will pay taxes when you take an income stream from your 401(k) once you are retired, but in the meantime your investments will grow tax deferred.

💰 Free money! Employer matching may be the best thing that ever happened to retirement savings. Many companies will match whatever contributions you make, up to a certain percentage, in order to attract and retain employees. Here's an example:

✓ Let's say that Jack makes $50,000 and has elected to contribute 5 percent of his annual salary to his 401(k) plan.

✓ Jack's company offers a 7 percent match.

✓ Each year, Jack contributes $2,500 (5 percent of his salary) to his 401(k) plan.

✓ Each year, Jack's company also contributes $2,500 (5 percent of his salary) to his 401(k) plan.

✓ The total yearly contribution made to Jack's plan is $5,000.

✓ Jack's company would be willing to match up to 7 percent of his salary (up to $3,500), but since he has only elected to contribute 5 percent, that is all his company will contribute.

I have to say, you would be crazy not to fund your 401(k) at least up to your company matching point. In Jack's case, he funds $2,500 and his company doubles it on Day 1. Where else can you make 100 percent rate of return on Day 1—guaranteed? But because Jack only contributes 5 percent of his salary ($2,500) instead of 7 percent ($3,500), he's walking away from $1,000 a year.

Keep in mind that while the money you contribute from your paycheck is always 100 percent yours, the funds your employer puts in usually vest over time. Call it an insurance policy against employees walking away from the company early. Once you're fully vested, you can take the entire company match with you when you say adios to your employer.

Leave before then, however, and you'll leave behind all that free money as well.

403(b)s

Employees of tax-exempt organizations, including nonprofit companies, religious groups, school districts and government organizations, can take advantage of 403(b) plans. These plans are basically the nonprofit equivalent to 401(k)s.

Whether your current job provides a 401(k) or a 403(b), take advantage of the many benefits you will receive both now and later by contributing into such a plan. The tougher you are on yourself today, the easier life will be on you later!

ROTH 401(k) AND ROTH 403(b)

I hope you're with me that participating in your employer's 401(k) or 403(b) plan is already a big step toward achieving your retirement goals. *Right?* But just as you have a choice between a traditional IRA and a Roth IRA when investing on your own, an increasing number of employers are offering a Roth option as part of their 401(k) and 403(b) plans.

Roth 401(k)s and Roth 403(b)s, which were introduced in 2006, combine the most advantageous components of the 401(k) with the Roth IRA.

At this point you're probably asking yourself, *What's the difference between a traditional and Roth 401(k)?*

Not surprisingly, the differences are comparable to the differences between traditional and Roth IRAs. It comes down to the timing of taxes you will need to pay. Would you rather pay taxes now or later? So, you have to ask yourself: Is your tax rate going to be higher or lower when you begin taking income from these accounts?

In a traditional 401(k), you contribute your income pre-tax and then pay taxes on the funds when you withdraw them during retirement. Switch to a Roth 401(k) and you pay the taxes up front so you can make withdrawals tax-free during retirement.

I'm often asked, *Which plan should I use?* I usually give an answer I learned from my dad: *Yes!*

If you think your tax rate will be higher when you retire than it currently is, go with the Roth 401(k) where your contributions will be taxed now, as you make them. Sure, that tax bite hurts. However, your distributions in retirement when you suspect your tax rate to be elevated will not be subject to any taxation at all.

If you believe your tax rate will be lower in the future, you'll want to fund a traditional 401(k) where you will not be taxed on your contributions now. Those contributions will be deducted from your federal income tax return, saving you taxes now. Future distributions will then be taxed during that period of life when you expect that your tax rate will be lower than it is today.

WHY NOT BET ON BOTH?

Both traditional and Roth 401(k) plans may have a place in your retirement portfolio. The good news is that you don't have to choose between them. As a matter of fact, if your employer offers both, the best move may be to opt for both.

In Chapter 5, I'll discuss the great benefits of diversification. But for now, since no one truly knows what taxes will look like with the current administration let alone 30 or 40 years into the future, why not hedge your bets? By implementing both a traditional 401(k) as well as a Roth 401(k), a part of your current taxable income will be decreased, you will sustain a diversified retirement plan, and you'll protect yourself if future tax rates change, which they probably will!

What if your employer doesn't offer a Roth 401(k)? If you're eligible, you can contribute to a Roth IRA in conjunction with your employer's traditional 401(k). In addition to the tax benefits, there's another advantage: You can withdraw your original contributions (not your gains) from a Roth IRA tax and penalty free. You can't do that with a Roth 401(k).

So far, we have discussed a number of "homes," a.k.a. retirement accounts, to house the investments that can be placed inside of them. These include:

✓	Traditional IRA	✓	403(b)
✓	Roth IRA	✓	Roth 401(k)
✓	401(k)	✓	Roth 403(b)

Before we start looking at the "furniture"—the actual investments you may want to furnish your accounts with—let's quickly discuss two additional accounts. These include SEP IRAs and SIMPLE IRAs, two different accounts with a focus on the self-employed.

SEP IRA

This acronym, which stands for Simplified Employee Pension, is a variation of a traditional IRA for self-employed individuals or small business owners. Any business owner with one or more employees can open and fund such an account. Contributions are tax deductible for the business and go into a traditional IRA held in the employee's name. If the self-employed person does have employees, all employees must receive the same benefits, which is why a SEP IRA is ideal when you (and your spouse) are the only employees. Like a traditional IRA, the money in a SEP IRA is not taxable until withdrawal.

One of the key advantages of a SEP IRA over a traditional or Roth IRA is the increased contribution limit. Since you can contribute up to 25 percent of your income or $54,000 (whichever is less), a SEP IRA can help successful business owners turbocharge their retirement account.

Another added benefit is that for a self-employed person with no employees, there are no significant administrative costs to get this plan up and running.

SIMPLE IRA

SIMPLE IRA stands for Savings Incentive Match Plan for Employees. It's similar to a SEP.

✓ Like a SEP, it's also a variation of a traditional IRA for small businesses and self-employed individuals.

✓ As with most traditional IRA and SEP plans, your contributions are tax deductible, and your investments grow tax deferred until you are ready to make withdrawals in retirement.

✓ They also allow for higher contribution limits than traditional or Roth IRAs—currently $12,500 along with an additional $3,000 in catch-up contributions if you have passed your 50th birthday.

✓ SIMPLE IRAs are straightforward to set up and easy to administer, and maintenance costs are low compared to 401(k) plans.

SIMPLE IRAs are like 401(k) plans for small businesses. Unlike SEP IRAs, SIMPLE IRAs give small employers the chance to provide their employees with a retirement plan that allows for employee contributions through salary reductions. But what truly makes a SIMPLE IRA distinctive is the employer is required to make a contribution on the employee's behalf. This can be either a dollar-for-dollar match of up to 3 percent of salary or a flat 2 percent of pay. This is required of the employer regardless of whether the employee contributes to their account.

In short, a SIMPLE IRA is a plan that gives smaller employers an easy way to contribute toward an employee's retirement account.

Now that you have a better sense of the different styles of investment homes available to you, whether you work for a company or are self-employed, let's take a look at a few styles of furniture, a.k.a. the investments, you can choose to furnish your investment homes. Individual stocks, mutual funds and ETFs are a good place to start. But first, we'll visit one of the friendliest and most beautiful places I have traveled to—Malawi, the warm heart of Africa—to show you that you *can* successfully jump into investing.

CHAPTER 4

WALKING ON WATER:
MAKING THE IMPOSSIBLE A REALITY

*Whatever the mind can conceive
and believe, it can achieve.*
—*Napoleon Hill*

I had never even heard of Malawi before arriving in Africa. Even though this heavily populated nation ranks among the world's least-developed and poorest countries, it didn't take long to realize that the friendly, welcoming, colorful and vibrant populace is Malawi's greatest asset. It's impossible to visit and not become engaged with the people who live there.

"Mzungu, Mzungu. What is your name?" the locals would exclaim again and again when I got off at a bus terminal or walked along the dirt road of any village. "Where are you from?"

"America," I would answer.

"America numba one!" they would exclaim. "Michael Jordan! Yeah!"

The greetings made me feel welcomed.

Surprisingly, I experienced this even at the Malawi border crossing, where welcoming immigration officers greeted me with smiles instead of the belligerent stares and the World War II vintage Kalashnikovs (better known around the globe as AK-47s) I had grown used to. To say that the soldiers at the other border crossings with their machine guns made me feel differently would be an understatement of monstrous proportions.

Indeed, the inhabitants' legendary friendliness has led to Malawi being called the warm heart of Africa, a label the country well and truly deserves.

About the size of Pennsylvania and surrounded by Mozambique, Zambia and Tanzania, this landlocked country is among the smallest on the continent. It's also one of the most scenic. I had heard that chilling out on golden sand beaches of its "inland sea," Lake Malawi, was a must. This 360-mile-long lake, which covers one fifth of the country, is Africa's third largest and home to over 1,000 different species of fish adorned in wild patterns of intense colors. I had to go.

How can there be tropical fish in a lake? I wondered once I got there. It was hard to fathom that it was not the ocean.

Malawi may seem like a backpacker's dream place to travel, but Lariam, the most powerful medication to prevent malaria, is not effective in this region. The thirsty female mosquitoes that spread this dreadful disease have developed a resistance to this prophylaxis. Simply taking the ineffective pharmaceutical is a challenge: It lives up to the warnings of hallucinations and vivid dreams listed on the bottle in fine print.

Fellow travelers Clay and Katherine from England were knocked flat as malaria's ferocious fever, headache, chills and vomiting set in. If left untreated, malaria can quickly become fatal. Fortunately, we had enough mefloquine and chloroquine to zap the progression of the disease and spare our friends. The same cannot be said for the villages, where the symptoms of malaria often get ignored. Even when properly diagnosed, most locals can't afford to spend the few dollars needed to buy medication. Sadly, almost a million people, mostly children under 5 years of age, die from malaria each year in Africa.

In all the 66 countries I have visited, I have never been more paranoid than I was in Malawi. I wasn't alone. It seemed like the African-ailment conversation was the most prevalent among fellow travelers. This was disastrous for our attitudes and morale as it caused minds to work overtime analyzing every cut, cough, crap, belch and bite. You hoped that you just had a case of the runs or the flu, but you couldn't shake the fear that you might have malaria, typhoid, yellow fever or even bilharzia, which is widely known to be ubiquitous in the lake.

You're probably asking yourself, *What in the world is bilharzia?* Well, it's not pleasant, but I'll tell you. Bilharzia is an illness caused by a nasty little worm that, like a lot of parasites, needs a host in which to lay its eggs. Guess who? That's right. Us. You can get infected by swimming in lakes where the freshwater has become contaminated by infected animal or human urine or feces. The parasites penetrate human skin to enter the bloodstream and then migrate to the liver, intestines and other organs where they start laying eggs. Locals warned us not to urinate in the lake as the parasite could enter your urethra. Yes, it's as gross as it sounds!

Symptoms of bilharzia can include a rash, itchy skin, fever, chills, cough, headache, belly pain, joint pain and muscle aches. An estimated 200 million people are infected with this parasite in Africa and 200,000 deaths are attributed to it annually. Even though bilharzia can be easily treated with medication, as you can imagine, I did not want to be exposed. I stayed on land.

Even so, the tropical lake with its pure white sand lapped by turquoise water and fringed by lush mountains under a sunny, blue sky reminded me of being on the beaches of Mo'orea, Tahiti. All I wanted to do was escape the extreme heat and humidity by diving into the water. This disappointment was the closest thing to sitting in a ski lodge in Alta, Utah, with a broken leg, looking out over two feet of fresh powder and sunny skies, and watching skiers celebrate their runs with high fives and beers in hand.

As I traveled from Nkhata Bay to Monkey Bay, the frustration of not swimming in the lake continued to mount. Days later, I arrived at Cape Maclear. The strip of idyllic beach was the social hub for the locals from Chembe Village. Some sections of the beach were full of activity with local fishermen and women filling up containers of water, while others were places the local children loved to play. The coming together of two different cultures, the tourist and the villager, proved to be just as joyful and rich.

Sunrise with the beautiful children, Lake Malawi

I found a pleasant place to stay called Mr. Steven's, which offered relatively clean grass bungalows on the beach for only 10 Kwacha per night. At the time, $1USD equated to 15 Kwacha. What a deal.

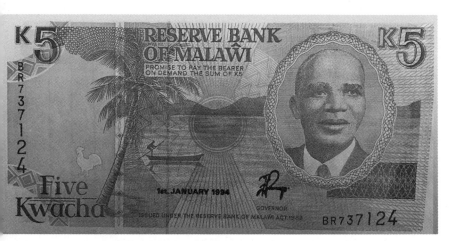

A 5-Kwacha note with a dugout canoe on Lake Malawi

I was surprised to see many travelers swimming in the lake. Many stated they had been enjoying the crystal-clear waters for weeks and had not gotten sick.

I've had enough, I said to myself. *I'm going in the damn lake!*

And that's exactly what I did. *Ahhh...* It felt so refreshing. I even remembered not to pee in the lake. When I finally exited the water, I decided to celebrate by purchasing an ice-cold Carlsberg at the thatched-roof bar. To my surprise, leaning against the side of this hut was a wooden water ski with bindings made of strips of leather. It could have dated back to 1922, the year water-skiing was invented. Having grown up water-skiing on Lake George in New York, I immediately thought how great it would be to water-ski on Lake Malawi. And that's when I started thinking, *Hmmm... The sport requires a smooth stretch of water—check! A water ski—check! A towboat with a towrope—not so lucky.*

"Do you know who owns the ski?" I asked the bartender.

He didn't. However, he did point to his friends Howard and Enoch who owned an aluminum rowboat equipped with a vintage Johnson outboard engine that appeared to be almost as old as the ski. Before I knew it, they were collaborating on how to make my dream become a reality.

Within minutes I was back in the placid water behind their boat, cord in hand. I knew it was not going to be easy for the 10-horsepower engine to get me up and out of the water, but I was determined to hold on for dear life. I kept my legs tucked into my chest in a cannonball position and the ski's tip out of the water, pointing toward the sky.

"Hit it!" I bellowed.

I leaned back and kept my legs slightly bent. The rowboat was struggling. I was struggling. Don't let go, I kept saying to myself. Don't let go. I did everything possible to hold on, when all of a sudden the ski began to plane and I was actually gliding over the water. I took in the scene and thought to myself how happy I was in that very moment. Howard and Enoch looked thrilled, but their expressions were nothing compared to those of the crowd that had gathered on the beach. The locals were pointing at me and jumping with joy. From their perspective, this Mzungu was performing the impossible by walking on water. They had never seen anything like it before. My ski had obviously just served as bar décor.

The crazy Mzungu walking on water, Lake Malawi, Africa

As the boat headed back toward the shore, I crossed the right wake, picking up enough speed to let go of the rope and coast up onto the beach. Did the kids think I was super human? All I knew as the locals swarmed me was that I had minimally used up five of my fifteen minutes of fame. Talk about fun! When things eventually quieted down, a woman brought me an enormous, fresh plate of rice, beans and fish as a way of saying *zikomo* (thank you) for the entertainment.

YOU CAN MAKE IT HAPPEN

Getting out of the water with a vintage wooden water ski behind a 10-horsepower engine strapped onto a rowboat is a similar analogy to a rocket ship launching into space, spending 80 percent of its fuel during takeoff and after a certain point flying smoothly with minimal consumption. The hardest part is just getting up.

Many millennials may think retirement is impossible. The people of Malawi thought walking on water was impossible, and frankly, when I saw the boat I would be behind I had to agree with them. You younger investors may feel like it's going to take a miracle to achieve your financial goals, but it's not. You don't need to walk on water. Successfully saving for retirement is not any different from water-skiing. You just have to understand what you are dealing with so you can put that knowledge to use. In short, you must understand the basics of investing and then make it happen by taking action today.

You can do this!

Riding the stock market is not all smooth sailing. There are highs, lows and things that, just like bilharzia, scare the crap out of you. But no matter how bad the markets get, they can't go up your urethra and kill you.

You already know the different types of investment homes from the last chapter. Your decisions about how to furnish the investment home you select are what will get you there. When you reach your goal, we'll celebrate with an ice-cold Carlsberg, rice, beans and fish. And you'll feel even more elated than I did when I skied on Lake Malawi.

So let's get you started furnishing your house by looking at three main investment vehicles:

- ✓ Stocks
- ✓ Mutual Funds
- ✓ ETFs

WHAT IS A STOCK?

Plain and simple, possessing a company's stock means that you are one of the many owners or shareholders of that company. The words *stock*, *equity* and *shares* all mean the same thing. A stock's price is determined on the open market by how much investors are willing to pay for it. This causes the price to rise or fall. Whether the stock is profitable depends largely upon the strength and continued success of the company in which you have invested.

If you were to purchase a share of Tesla, you would immediately become a part owner of this inspiring electric car manufacturer. Does this mean you can get a discount on a new Model 3 or enjoy a free lunch at the employee cafeteria? Sorry, but the answer would be a resounding no, because your ownership stake would be quite small. Even so, there is opportunity.

Here are some of the benefits to owning individual stocks:

 Profits: As an owner, you're entitled to your share of the company's earnings, which means that you have a claim to a piece of the profits the company generates. When Tesla went public in 2010, its stock was selling for $17 per share. By 2017 it was selling for over $200 per share. Each share has grown by more than 12 times. Not a bad return in seven years!

$ Dividends: These are payments given to shareholders from the company's earnings. The amount is decided by the board of directors and is based on what portion of earnings they feel should be reinvested into the company to achieve sustained growth for the future and what portion should be allocated to shareholders as a reward for being a part owner of the company. Not all companies have a history of paying dividends regularly—this is certainly the case with most younger, growing companies, such as Tesla, because the reinvestment of their capital is essential for continued research, development and growth. For this reason, dividends tend to come from more established companies with solid cash flow.

$ Low Costs: Owning individual stocks is less expensive than owning mutual funds and ETFs. Mutual funds charge fees to cover their overhead or operating expenses, which include management, administration, distribution, marketing and record keeping. These fees are expressed as a percentage of assets in the fund and are commonly known as an expense ratio. The average mutual fund charges 1.25 percent per year; however, owning an individual stock means no annual cost to you. Lower costs can lead to higher returns.

💰 Taxes: As you'll find out in the next section on mutual funds, in a taxable account you will pay taxes every year on your portion of the capital gains generated by that fund. This does not happen when you own individual stocks. Also, by owning stocks individually you have greater flexibility when it comes to tax-loss harvesting (the practice of selling a security that has experienced a loss to offset taxes on a stock you sold with gains). If you own a mutual fund, even if some of the fund's holdings had a loss, the fund itself might have a gain. By owning individual stocks, you're able to realize the individual losses, whether short term or long term, for tax purposes.

💰 Voting Rights: You will typically receive one vote for each share of stock you own, enabling you to vote on issues such as election of a board of directors and other important issues affecting the direction of the company. This means you do get some say in the management of the company, even though they don't know your name.

💰 Support Your Companies: When you own a company's stock, you probably want to be their client. If you own shares of Verizon, for example, you may be more likely to use their cellphone service since that means you're supporting a company you own. So every time you pay your monthly fee, you'll know you could be helping to fund your annual dividend check.

With all of these great benefits, why do so many investors today choose to own mutual funds or today's new charmer, ETFs? When it comes right down to it, you probably don't have the time, inclination or resources to investigate individual stocks thoroughly enough to make good choices and you'd probably rather be surfing, skiing or camping in the great outdoors, or even reading a good book. If you're like most investors, you have probably not studied financial economics, read financial journals or books on the Modern Portfolio Theory, which I'll talk about in the next chapter. That's why you could end up, like most investors, with a portfolio that isn't properly diversified, tracked and rebalanced. So, why not leave it to the fund managers at the mutual fund or ETF companies who are much better equipped to actively choose for you?

I equate stocks to that vintage wooden water ski and aluminum rowboat with the 10-horsepower Johnson outboard. All that equipment did work; however, with advancements in technology and materials, these days there may be more effective ways to get the job done.

Let's first take a look at mutual funds.

WHAT IS A MUTUAL FUND?

A mutual fund is an investment strategy that enables you to pool your money together with thousands of other investors to purchase an assortment of stocks, bonds or other securities that would be challenging to reconstruct on your own. They are run by money managers who construct portfolios after significant research, with the goal of creating profits for those who invest into their mutual funds. Each shareholder partakes proportionally in the gain or loss of the fund.

Here's why mutual funds have been so popular over the years:

💰 Professional Management: Investors purchase funds because they do not have the time, interest or expertise to manage their own investment portfolios. Can you relate? A mutual fund offers small investors access to professionally managed portfolios in a relatively inexpensive manner.

💰 Simplicity: Purchasing a mutual fund is straightforward and the minimum investment is small. As little as $100 a month can be invested with most fund companies. Mutual funds can be purchased directly through mutual fund companies, at your bank or with the guidance of a financial advisor.

💰 Diversification: If you're interested in diversification (a risk management technique that mixes a wide variety of investments within a portfolio) just wait until the next chapter when I take you on an ultralight flight to illustrate why it's important to both maintain perspective and mitigate risk. For now, however, let's focus on mutual funds. When you own shares in such a fund instead of individual stocks or bonds, your risk is spread out. Mutual funds often own hundreds of different stocks or bonds. The more of those you have inside the fund, the less any one of them can hurt you. Just think of companies such as Kodak or Enron that used to be huge and now no longer exist. If your entire portfolio had been invested into Enron (see the story in Chapter 7), you would have lost everything in 2001. In contrast, even though almost all large-cap mutual funds (those mutual funds that focus on companies with market capitalization greater than $5 billion) owned Enron stock, you would have lost less than 1 percent of your portfolio's value.

§ Liquidity: As with individual stocks, mutual funds let you exchange your investments into cash in a fast and uncomplicated way.

§ Economies of Scale: Mutual funds buy and sell large amounts of securities at a time, enabling the transaction costs to be far less expensive than what you would pay for such securities transactions.

I have been investing in mutual funds since I was in college in order to take advantage of all the benefits shared in this section. Back then I skied on the best water ski of the day, made of graphite, and did so behind a 22-foot fiberglass Sea Ray with a 225-horsepower inboard engine. But what if there was something better? Today there are both better skis and better boats, just as there are better investment vehicles for your financial future. Before we explore those, however, I want to introduce you to Peaches.

Peaches is my 1956 Morris Minor convertible. I purchased her in 2001, shortly after moving to beautiful Bend, Oregon. I drive her to work most summer days and somehow when I'm behind the wheel, which is located on the English (right) side, any worries or concerns have a way of evaporating into the heavens.

Driving Peaches, my 1956 Morris Minor, Mt. Bachelor, Oregon

Peaches has brought a continual stream of serendipity into my life and I consider her a dear friend. For the better part of a decade, she was the face of my financial practice as her non-ostentatious, adventurous spirit shared a message about the road to financial independence. It was as though she said:

Envision your life's journey.
See yourself in the driver's seat.
Make the right turns on your financial journey.

Peaches may have a tremendous amount of charm, but at her age she obviously does not have an anti-lock brake system, better known as ABS, which was created to prevent car brakes from locking up and leading to uncontrolled skidding. As those of us who live in Central Oregon know all too well, it's a nerve-wracking event trying to stop a car in a hurry on a slippery road. ABS eliminates much of this challenge. These new brakes started to become a standard feature in high-end luxury cars in the early '90s. Today, you'd be hard-pressed to find any automobile manufacturer that does not install them in all their cars as this innovative system saves countless lives each and every year.

Now if you were to ask me whether the old braking system in Peaches is bad, I would have to say *no*. Even though she has already celebrated her 60th birthday, her brakes work great. I apply pressure and she comes to a rather quick stop. That being said, would I ever purchase a new model car today without ABS? No!

I feel a similar way about purchasing mutual funds today. Yes, they work very well and provide significant benefits, which I previously discussed. However, the newest innovative investments are called ETFs, short for Exchange Traded Funds, which in my opinion just work a little (or a lot) better.

WHY ETFs?

Choosing between mutual funds and ETFs is like choosing between any two entities involved in an age-old rivalry. Think of the Yankees and the Red Sox, Coke and Pepsi or PC vs. Mac. In this case, the rivalry is between active versus passive investing.

"It's $900 to fix the brakes ...or $10
to make the horn louder."

Active management refers to a strategy in which money managers make specific investment decisions with the goal of outperforming an investment benchmark. The challenge is that most actively managed mutual funds fail to beat their benchmarks. What does this mean? Let's say you purchased a large-cap mutual fund that owns a combination of stocks from companies with large market capitalization. The fund manager and its shareholders will compare its annual performance to that of the S&P 500 Index—or "the S&P," as many refer to this American stock market index of 500 large companies that have their stock listed on the exchange. At the end of any given year, a majority of large-cap mutual fund managers have not outperformed the S&P's average. Sad but true.

In fact, while investors have historically relied upon actively managed mutual funds to achieve diversification and asset allocation, most actively managed mutual funds have underperformed market indices over time. Studies show that 80 percent of the more expensive actively managed mutual funds fail to beat their benchmarks. *S&P Indices Versus Active* funds scorecard, an annual study performed by Standard & Poor's, shared that a majority of equity funds were outperformed by their respective index or benchmark over the last one-, three- and five-year periods. In addition, Morningstar found that in 2015, most active managers underperformed their respective indexes in seven out of nine categories of mutual funds.

Similar statistics date back for decades. This greatly bothered John Bogle, the founder and retired CEO of the Vanguard Group. So in 1975 he developed an innovative idea. *Since most managers will not reach or surpass their benchmark, why not have a strategy that tracks the returns of a specific market index as closely as possible by holding all or a representative selection of securities in the index?* he thought to himself. So he created the world's first index mutual fund.

His core belief was that it's close to impossible to beat the market through stock selection or market timing over an extended period. The managers who may accomplish that feat this year will probably not do so next year, and have never been able to do so over many years. Bogle feels that buying and selling securities with the intention of outperforming the market is purely a game of chance, and that indexing eliminates the risk that an active manager will select securities that underperform the market. This summarizes the passive or index approach to investing.

Today, ETFs provide an efficient, low-cost way to implement such a passive strategy. Most ETFs track an index. In 1993, State Street Global Advisors brought to market the first ETF called the SPDR, pronounced "spider." This enabled investors to trade the entire S&P 500 in a single share of stock. Today, ETFs are listed on a variety of exchanges, may trade on all major stock exchanges both domestic and global, and track nearly every index you can imagine. Bogle and his company Vanguard followed suit shortly thereafter, and today rank second in worldwide ETF sales.

As the world's fastest-growing investment vehicle, Lipper reports that ETFs continue to outpace the competing mutual fund industry. The numbers speak for themselves. In 2004, there were only about 150 ETFs; by 2017, there were almost

2,000. And since the year 2000, the increase in assets invested into ETFs has grown by over 2,500 percent, compared to an increase of only 120 percent for mutual funds. The ETF industry has set a new record for global asset gathering, with assets totaling nearly $2.5 trillion by 2017. Keep in mind that this is still only a dent in the roughly $16 trillion mutual fund industry. Still, the trend is quite clear. ETFs are fast becoming the vehicle of choice for investment advisors and investors who have noticeably been choosing to move money toward passive investment strategies and away from active.

SO WHAT ARE THE BENEFITS OF ETFs?

I believe the growth of ETFs has been so remarkable because they uniquely combine the benefits of stocks and mutual funds into one seamless vehicle. Let's first take a look at the advantageous traits ETFs have over owning individual stocks.

💰 LOW COST

Helping investors save money is where ETFs really shine, as it's not what you make but what you keep that counts. Similar to mutual funds, ETFs charge a fee to cover their overhead. Since index investment managers don't actively attempt to outperform a given market by betting on individual stocks, there is no need for a very costly team of market analysts. This leads to much lower expense ratios than mutual funds. Today, an average equity mutual fund charges 1.25 percent in expenses. The average ETF carries an expense ratio of only 0.25 percent.

The noteworthy difference of 1 percent in fees between an average mutual fund and ETF will make an enormous difference in your profitability over time. Fees are part of doing business with investment companies; however, the bottom line is that ETFs enable you to keep more of what you earn.

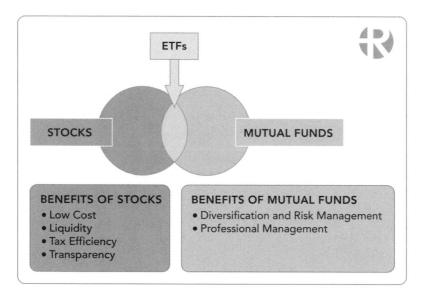

💰 LIQUIDITY

Since ETFs, like stocks, are traded throughout the day, ETFs allow for liquidation of a position faster than a mutual fund. In contrast, mutual fund shares are bought and sold directly with the fund company and are priced just once a day after the markets have closed. So while ETFs provide the flexibility to get into or out of a position at any time throughout the day, this is not the case with mutual funds.

As we've experienced in recent history, the stock market indexes can quickly climb and abruptly plunge in a single trading day. For some investors, having the ability to trade at a moment's notice rather than wait until the end of the day to adjust one's investments is a significant benefit.

💰 TAX EFFICIENCY

ETFs have become one of the most tax-efficient investment vehicles for investors. Even though the same tax rules apply to ETFs and mutual funds, ETFs are renowned for having low portfolio turnover, especially in comparison to an actively managed portfolio.

Okay, I'm about to throw yet another term at you: *turnover*. Assume that a mutual fund has $100 million in assets under management, and the portfolio manager sells $30 million in securities during the year. The rate of turnover is $30 million divided by $100 million or 30 percent. Portfolios that are actively managed usually have a higher turnover rate, which creates greater capital gains distributions as well as trading costs, thus reducing the returns in the portfolio.

The tax efficiency of ETFs is further enhanced because ETF investors are protected from the trading activity of fellow shareholders. Unfortunately for mutual fund investors, mutual fund managers are frequently forced to liquidate portfolio holdings to meet the redemption demands of fleeing shareholders. The remaining fund shareholders are negatively impacted as they must absorb the tax gains and/or possible losses triggered by such inopportune transactions. ETFs dodge this dilemma because they are bought and sold on an exchange, which means that investors have no impact on each other's tax consequences.

💰 TRANSPARENCY

You can't know what you own if a fund does not tell you what it owns. Both ETFs and mutual funds hold many different stocks and bonds. When you purchase an ETF, you're clearly able to see the entire holdings of your ETF by going to their company website. Since ETFs disclose their portfolio holdings daily, you get complete transparency and full knowledge of exactly what you are buying.

Mutual funds, on the other hand, only report their holdings on a quarterly or semiannual basis. This lack of information can create challenges when you want to base important investment decisions on the financial facts.

MORE ETF ADVANTAGES

Mutual funds certainly have noteworthy qualities that ETFs have borrowed. Let's get a better understanding of those as well.

💰 DIVERSIFICATION AND RISK MANAGEMENT

You may already know the drill on diversification, and I'll explain it further in the next chapter. For now, let's just say that the more securities you own in an asset class, the more protected you may be when any one of those securities takes a nose dive. ETFs are designed to track an index that represents an asset class such as large-cap, international equities, bonds, etc. To accomplish this on your own, you would have to invest in many, many, many different holdings from a particular asset class. With a single trade, an ETF lets you instantly achieve index-like diversification of an entire index. There are ETFs to cover every major index, asset class and niche that an investor can imagine. An entire portfolio of diversified investments can be created quickly and simply by using ETFs. This investment tool even offers direct exposure to assets like currencies, real estate and natural resources such as gold and oil. As pooled investments, I believe ETFs expand diversification and ultimately lower risk.

💰 PROFESSIONAL MANAGEMENT

As with mutual funds, you don't have to keep track of every single investment your ETF owns. Both mutual funds and ETFs are managed by experts who take care of that for you. Almost every one of today's major indexes has an ETF that invests into it. These ETFs are passively managed by an investment or trust company. These companies take on the responsibility of maintaining the collection of stocks within the index to which they are associated. The company then converts the portfolio into individual shares of ETFs, which are then traded on the stock exchange like regular stocks.

Part of the maintenance of the portfolio entails the collection and safekeeping of dividends paid by companies within the index portfolio. It is the duty of the trust companies to distribute these payments to the ETF stockholders.

Earlier, I equated stocks to the vintage boat and water ski I used on Lake Malawi. Sure, they worked, but consider the advances. Guided by the principles of physics and hydrodynamics as well as years of design experience, water ski manufacturers are on a continual quest to craft the most advanced ski possible.

I believe ETFs are the investment equivalent of today's top-of-the-line water ski. Made of carbon, the superior ski is durable, fast, lightweight and has comfortable neoprene bindings. This ski is designed to track well and effortlessly floats over wakes. Let's also not forget today's state-of-the-art Malibu Wakesetter 23 LSV boat equipped with a 450-horsepower engine that whips you out of the water in a matter of seconds.

In short, we've come a long way from the days of wooden skis with leather straps and an aluminum rowboat. Investments have made a similar leap, witness ETFs.

PHEW!

You now have a background regarding some of the main types of financial accounts or "homes" (IRAs, Roth IRAs, 401(k)s, etc.) that are available to you as well as some key investments or "furniture" (stocks, mutual funds, ETFs) that you may place inside of these investment homes. Good job! Give yourself a high five. As with furnishing your home, you can always combine different styles of modern, rustic, traditional, etc. There is nothing wrong with owning some stocks, mutual funds and ETFs to furnish your investment homes.

Even if this all makes sense to you, you're probably asking yourself: *How do I best diversify my own portfolio? How do I best ensure that I do not make mistakes?* While those strategies may be a lot easier than you think, they're often helped along by having a completely new and different perspective. How better to achieve this than from 1,000 feet above the ground in an ultralight?

That's next.

CHAPTER 5

THE UNLUCKIEST GENERATION: A NEW FINANCIAL PERSPECTIVE

When nothing goes right ... go left.

As far as current events are concerned, 2008 was another busy year. Cuba's Fidel Castro retired after 49 years in power. The New York Giants defeated the New England Patriots in the Super Bowl. Michael Phelps swam away with eight gold medals in the Beijing Olympics. Barack Obama was elected president of the United States.

Oh yeah. And Americans, along with much of the world, experienced the worst economic downturn in nearly a century. Not only that, but it was the worst year for the U.S. stock market—ever.

It has been said that timing is everything. If you are a millennial who just happened to be graduating from college and looking to start your career in the depths of the Great

Recession, you were most likely knocked flat on your back before you even had a solid footing. Talk about being cursed with unfortunate career timing. That had to be a serious shock to you and your entire graduating class. These experiences during such impressionable years have led many millennials to take an emotionally driven approach to financial planning and to adopt conservative money habits that many compare to the investment behavior of young adults during the Great Depression.

ADULTHOOD DEFERRED

Nothing could have prepared you graduates for the economic sledgehammer that followed the collapse of the world's stock and housing market, which began in December 2007 and ended in June 2009. The financial markets were under siege and no one in their wildest dreams could have ever imagined that the world's largest mortgage company, insurance company, stock brokerage firm, investment bank and savings and loans would have all declared bankruptcy or no longer exist. I would have thought you were delirious if you had told me this was possible before the impossible became a reality. For crying out loud, even the world's largest automaker—GM—went bankrupt. It wasn't the only company that got thrashed. Chrysler, previously one of the big three U.S. automakers, is now owned by the Italians.

In all likelihood, your parents and/or grandparents had a financial plan, probably a really good plan. But $hit happens; 2008 is proof of that. Good people—maybe your own parents, who had worked hard and accomplished much—lost homes and retirement accounts. Many retirees, maybe your grandparents, were forced to return to work.

I try to imagine what it must have been like to start your career during this ominous time. Like most new graduates, you probably felt that the possibilities were endless when you got out of college. It likely did not take long to become totally disenfranchised.

A couple of years after I graduated from college, I moved out of my parents' house and rented a room in my friend Greg Murphy's home, which meant buying my own food and clothes along with watching endless *Seinfeld* episodes. Then my dad called me into his home office and told me it was time for me to assume the payments for my health insurance.

"You're no longer part of our plan," he said. "So this is on you now."

"What do you mean health insurance is on me?" I exclaimed.

This expensive endeavor of setting out on my own had just become even pricier. I didn't love the reality check, but I was determined to remain independent. So I sucked it up and found a way to cover my health insurance payments along with everything else.

In the past, entering adulthood logically led to moving out, getting married, having children, buying a house—all the trappings and expenses of a middle-class lifestyle. But today, a larger portion of you millennials are moving back in with your parents and uttering *no thanks*—or at least *not yet*—when it comes to tying the knot and having children of your own. Are these ramifications of the economic times? I believe so.

My intention is not to relive the shocking headlines of the past or even delve deep into the well-documented corporate greed that led to an excess of undisciplined lending to unqualified borrowers. I suggest reading the book or watching the movie *The Big Short*, which effectively explains in an uncomplicated and sometimes comedic format how subprime loans were turned into financial instruments that were then bought and sold by Wall Street institutions. Eventually, these super-risky subprime loans ended up on the balance sheets of major U.S. investment banks as well as becoming a significant part of the investment portfolios inside our 401(k)s and IRAs.

Who would have ever imagined that Wall Street's lack of scruples could so directly impact us? Many economists believe that you millennials are a generation whose daunting experiences will beleaguer you for the rest of your working lives. I believe by gaining knowledge of the sound financial principles contained in this book—along with learning how to keep your emotions at bay and not be immobilized by fear (my least favorite word)—you will become the generation that pushes the economy forward.

Still, I get how easy it would be after such an experience to hide money under your mattress, never buy a house—or buy the world's smallest one, if you subscribe to the idea of the tiny house movement. It's all about your perspective.

A DIFFERENT PERSPECTIVE FROM ABOVE

It's easier to embrace a different perspective when you keep climbing to a unique vantage point. At the age of 12, that vantage point was the seat of my father's bright orange Ariens riding lawn mower. I would often volunteer to mow my parents' lawn, since that gave me the opportunity to drive something with a motor and four wheels. This was the closest experience to driving a car for a raring-to-go pre-teen.

I was fastidious for a kid and did my best to make the lawn look like Yankee Stadium, complete with precise, crisscrossed lines. Could it be that I'm a Virgo? This penchant for precision would help me with my two careers—sealing driveways and managing my clients' wealth.

I have to admit I'm pretty thankful that Fred Rafilson, my friend and hometown expert ultralight pilot, shares this same trait.

As KTVZ news anchor Bob Shaw always says, it was a sparkling morning in Central Oregon. The wind was nonexistent when we taxied down the runway at the Prineville Airport on a contraption that somehow reminded me of Dad's riding lawn mower. I could never have imagined that one day someone would place a 30-foot wing atop a similar piece of equipment, relocate the blade behind the driver and fly high in the sky.

Getting ready for takeoff in Fred Rafilson's ultralight
Prineville, Oregon

Once we had been cleared, it took only seconds for this powered hang glider with its three-wheeled undercarriage and 50-horsepower engine to reach a speed of 32 mph. Effortlessly we took flight, our steep climb immediately offering a most spectacular view and different perspective of the area I thought I knew so well.

Once I eased into my new surroundings, Fred pointed out some the local landmarks, including the new Facebook Data Center. I spotted the Crooked River and instantly understood how it had procured its name. I looked out over vast, verdant fields of alfalfa and farmhouses that reminded me of Kansas.

My heart started to beat faster as we approached Smith Rock, a sanctuary of majestic rock spires that serves as an outdoor playground to me and other rock-climbing enthusiasts. As we flew adjacent to the towering walls of Phoenix Buttress, over Misery Ridge and on to Monkey Face, fears of being blown against the cliff face surfaced.

Remain calm, I told myself.

I knew that only by controlling my emotions and my thoughts could I help ensure a safe return.

The same lesson applies to investing, a notion I share with my clients on a continual basis. The current stock market volatility is often a very emotional experience for investors. Heck, if I had been introduced to investing after entering the work world at a time of market collapse, I might never have started. However, over-investing in emotions is bad news when it comes to financial success. So, I want to help you take a different point of view.

A LITTLE HISTORY

I believe it's crucial to be invested in the markets if your goal is to be independent of a paycheck one day. However, it's important to have a good understanding of how the markets historically work. It never ceases to amaze me how violently and rapidly the market can move in both directions. According to Yardeni Research, Inc., since 1946, there have been 11 bear markets where the market decline has exceeded 20 percent. The average decline has been 35 percent. When you observe the many economic challenges our country currently faces, I suggest asking yourself, "Haven't we had some of these situations in one form or another for the past 50 years?"

I can remember my parents sitting in gas lines when I was a young child during the oil embargo, as well as when inflation rose above 13 percent in 1980—the year the first millennials were born.

You probably remember the dot-com crash shortly after 9/11. Then there was the financial calamity of 2008. Who can forget that?

We've survived these and many other financial challenges on an irregular basis for half a century. I suspect we will continue to encounter turbulent air as we pilot our way through our lifetimes. Even factors like Russia's Vladimir Putin, North Korea's Kim Jong-un, Syria's Bashar al-Assad, China's economic slowdown and the U.S.'s absurd politics can prove challenging to the economy.

The worst move one can make in the middle of such turbulence is to get tense or even bail off the ultralight. All too often, however, that's exactly what investors do.

Many investors abandon long-term strategies for the perceived safety of cash. This can leave a hole in your savings that never really gets repaired. That's exactly what happened to thousands of investors on October 19, 1987, that ominous date known as Black Monday. The almost 23 percent plunge was the largest one-day percentage decline in stock market history. The Dow Jones Industrial Average (DJIA), a price-weighted average of 30 large companies on the New York Stock Exchange, dropped by 508 points to 1,739. Investors thought the end was near and panic set in throughout the financial world. Interestingly, the DJIA not only ended that year in positive territory, it closed on December 31, 1987, at an all-time record high of 1,939 points.

WHERE DID THE BULL AND BEAR MARKET GET THEIR NAMES?

Bulls are known to be aggressive and spirited while bears are considered to be slower and sluggish.

This is why a bull market occurs when prices are increasing and a bear market refers to a market in which prices decline.

Another explanation derives from the way in which each animal attacks its opponents. A bull will thrust its horns up into the air, while a bear will swipe its paws with a downward motion.

Here's a little secret. There has never been a down stock or real estate market that has not rebounded to hit an all-time high!

Today, the DJIA can fluctuate in a single trading day by as much as Black Monday's 508 points. If someone had told you back then that on January 25, 2017, the DJIA would surpass

20,000, up over 300 percent from 2009 levels, you would have thought they had lost their senses. That's a serious rebound, to say the least, in just eight years.

The economy will more than likely continue its undulating movements. But history shows us that chances are you'll have more savings to build on if you stay the course. That's certainly not easy to do. The secret? Instead of declaring war with your emotions, develop a diversified long-term strategy and stick to it.

FOCUS, FOCUS, FOCUS

Sticking to the plan isn't the easiest thing to do, especially when you're also having to do battle with your feelings. The Rule of 72—one of the handiest and most impressive financial formulas I learned early on—can help you focus on what counts: your long-term investment goal.

Kin Hubbard stated:

> The safest way to double your money is to fold it over and put it in your pocket.

However, the Rule of 72 is the easiest way to approximate how quickly your money will double at a given rate of return. Here's how it works:

Simply divide 72 by the annual rate of return you expect on your investment. Let's say you invest $25,000 in an investment earning a hypothetical 6 percent annually. Per the equation, (72 ÷ 6 = 12), your investment would double to ap-proximately $50,000 in 12 years. This formula works for any type of investment. If you purchased a home and its value increased by 8 percent a year, it would only take approxi-mately nine years to double the value of your investment (72 ÷ 8 = 9).

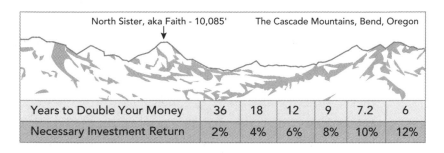

North Sister, aka Faith - 10,085'   The Cascade Mountains, Bend, Oregon

Years to Double Your Money	36	18	12	9	7.2	6
Necessary Investment Return	2%	4%	6%	8%	10%	12%

The simple things are usually what make a big impact on our lives. After learning the Rule of 72, I was motivated at a young age to live below my means, save money to invest and begin to experience the powers of compound interest.

Let's face it, money is very emotional. It's emotional in a great way when we're making lots of it and twice as emotional when we're losing it—even if it's only a paper loss. That's why we need to use every trick in the book to make sure we're playing it smart where our finances are concerned. When it comes to investing, playing it smart can be summed up in a single word: *diversification*.

DIVERSIFICATION

For those of you who aren't familiar with the concept of diversification, here's the definition of the word *diversify*.

> *To make diverse: give variety to. To balance (as an investment portfolio) defensively by dividing funds among securities of different industries or of different classes.*

So far so good. But what does the term *diversified portfolio* mean?

Diversified portfolio is one of the most powerful investment concepts to grasp and apply. All it really means is that you save and place your eggs (or investments) in different baskets that perform well under different market conditions.

By placing your money in an assortment of investments or asset classes that have little correlation to each other, you increase the likelihood that when some of your investments are down, others will be up.

As the term *asset classes* is commonplace in the world of investing, let's get a better understanding of what it means. An asset class is a group of securities that share similar traits and characteristics and thus behave in the same way out there in the real world.

I know we've likened the various types of retirement accounts—IRAs, 401(k)s, etc.—to a house, and stocks, mutual funds and ETFs to the furniture you can place in that house.

But just as there are huge variations in the style of furniture you select for your living room or bedroom, there are many subsets of asset classes to choose from. As we explore this further, please bear with me as I switch gears (and metaphors) to help explain.

I live near a boutique shop called Newport Market. They are well known for having an incredible variety of fresh, organic produce that is presented in a very attractive manner. If you were to invest in grapefruit, oranges and kiwis as well as kale, corn and carrots, your broad asset classes would be considered fruits and vegetables. However, fueling your body with just two asset classes wouldn't be great for your health. You might want to add additional foods like meat, poultry, fish, nuts and grains to balance your diet. Similarly, to be financially healthy we need to diversify our financial asset classes.

Each asset class can be partitioned into subclasses. Stocks can be broken down by industry, location, size and whether they are growth or value stocks. Let's take a look at some examples.

✓ **Industry:** Is the company in energy, information, technology, manufacturing, automotive, etc.?

✓ **Location:** Is the company based in the U.S. or overseas? If it's a foreign company, is it in a country with developed economies or emerging markets, i.e. a country with a relatively undeveloped economy? Companies located here are considered to be more volatile and risky, thus larger returns are expected. The largest emerging stock markets are located in the BRIC countries (Brazil, Russia, India and China).

✓ **Size:** Larger companies tend to be more stable and less risky than younger, smaller ones, like startups. Smaller companies can have a lot more growth potential along with that risk. That's why it's worthwhile to invest in a mix of cap sizes. Those include:

- **Large-Cap:** A company whose value exceeds about $5 billion. Think Exxon and Wal-Mart.

- **Mid-Cap:** A company whose market value is between about $1 billion and $5 billion.

- **Small-Cap:** A company whose market value is typically less than $1 billion. Most of these companies you haven't heard of unless they're located in your hometown.

- **Micro-Cap:** A very small company, often less than $300 million.

✓ **Growth vs. Value:** Each stock, regardless of its industry, location or size, can be branded as either a growth or value stock.

Growth investors focus on industries with strong momentum as an indication of the market's confidence in a company's ability to continue increasing earnings at an above-average pace. Take Apple with its iPhones. The company's stock is expensive relative to earnings, but investors think the price is justified by high potential for future growth.

Value investors seek stocks that appear to be undervalued by the marketplace, i.e. a stock that is lower in price relative to earnings and dividends. For example, there's usually not much expectation that Procter & Gamble's stock price will skyrocket anytime soon, but investors are happy to hold it because of the low downside risk and high dividends.

✓ **Blend:** A mix of the two.

💰 When diversifying a portfolio, it is crucial to have investments spread across all or most of the different asset classes. Investing in only one asset class is proverbially putting all of your eggs in one basket.

DIFFERENT STROKES

Feeling confused? While this diversification stuff may seem overwhelming, all you really need to remember is to include a broad mix of asset classes in your portfolio. I can make this even easier to understand by introducing you to my daughter Sophie and my son Jack.

Sophie and Jack come from the same parents and yet they behave very differently from one another. Without any guidance, Sophie had an affinity as a young girl to the color pink, Barbie dolls and Dora, while Jack gravitated to yellow Tonka Trucks, baseball and skateboards.

Like my children, investment asset classes come from the same parents and yet they can—and do—behave very differently.

My clients and I always get a kick out of the Callan Periodic Table of Investment Returns. In a rather amusing yet informative way, the chart below illustrates the historic returns of nine of the 24 essential asset classes from 2006 to 2016. In each of the years, one asset class is the winner and one is the loser. Let's focus on U.S. government bonds for this example. In 2006, the worst-performing asset class experienced a +2.67 percent return for the year. By 2008, that same asset class was the best performer, only to become the worst performer once again in 2009. By 2011, it had returned to the top position only to nose-dive back to the bottom in 2012. In 2014 and 2015, investors were giving up on natural resources, but look where that asset class was in 2016.

In short, individual asset classes bounce all over the place as they behave differently under different economic conditions. Come to think of it, certain people you and I know bounce all over the place and behave very differently under different conditions!

Stocks and bonds can often yield wide-ranging results. Investing in a mix of these different asset classes can improve the performance of your overall portfolio, cushioning your retirement savings against price swings in one asset class. This can be an effective way to weather the twists and turns that ever-changing market conditions can throw at your investments.

CALENDAR YEAR RETURNS

2006	2007	2008	2009	2010	2011	2012	2013	2014	2015	2016
REAL ESTATE 35.50%	EMERGING MARKET 39.39%	US GOV'T BONDS 2.67%	EMERGING MARKET 78.51%	REAL ESTATE 26.93%	US GOV'T BONDS 15.59%	REAL ESTATE 18.93%	SMALL CAP STOCKS 41.31%	REAL ESTATE 27.24%	REAL ESTATE 2.14%	NATURAL RESOURCES 30.87%
EMERGING MARKET 32.17%	NATURAL RESOURCES 34.44%	US CORP BONDS 0.96%	MID-CAP STOCKS 37.38%	MID-CAP STOCKS 26.64%	US CORP BONDS 9.15%	EMERGING MARKET 18.22%	MID-CAP STOCKS 33.50%	LARGE CAP STOCKS 13.69%	US GOV'T BONDS 1.76%	SMALL CAP STOCKS 26.56%
FOREIGN STOCKS 26.34%	FOREIGN STOCKS 11.17%	SMALL CAP STOCKS -31.07%	NATURAL RESOURCES 37.54%	SMALL CAP STOCKS 26.31%	REAL ESTATE 6.05%	MID-CAP STOCKS 17.88%	LARGE CAP STOCKS 32.39%	MID-CAP STOCKS 9.77%	LARGE CAP STOCKS 1.38%	MID-CAP STOCKS 20.74%
NATURAL RESOURCES 16.85%	US GOV'T BONDS 10.20%	MID-CAP STOCKS -36.23%	FOREIGN STOCKS 31.78%	NATURAL RESOURCES 23.88%	LARGE CAP STOCKS 2.11%	FOREIGN STOCKS 17.32%	FOREIGN STOCKS 22.78%	US CORP BONDS 8.06%	US CORP BONDS -0.74%	LARGE CAP STOCKS 11.96%
LARGE CAP STOCKS 15.79%	MID-CAP STOCKS 7.9%	LARGE CAP STOCKS -37.00%	REAL ESTATE 30.81%	EMERGING MARKET 18.88%	SMALL CAP STOCKS 1.02%	SMALL CAP STOCKS 16.33%	NATURAL RESOURCES 16.49%	SMALL CAP STOCKS 5.76%	FOREIGN STOCKS -0.81%	EMERGING MARKET 11.19%
SMALL CAP STOCKS 15.12%	LARGE CAP STOCKS 5.49%	REAL ESTATE -40.07%	LARGE CAP STOCKS 26.46%	LARGE CAP STOCKS 15.06%	MID-CAP STOCKS -1.73%	LARGE CAP STOCKS 16.00%	REAL ESTATE 1.77%	US GOV'T BONDS 3.22%	SMALL CAP STOCKS -2.00%	REAL ESTATE 7.56%
MID-CAP STOCKS 10.32%	US CORP BONDS 4.01%	NATURAL RESOURCES -42.55%	SMALL CAP STOCKS 25.57%	US CORP BONDS 9.37%	NATURAL RESOURCES -7.35%	US CORP BONDS 11.85%	US GOV'T BONDS -1.97%	EMERGING MARKET -2.19%	MID-CAP STOCKS -2.18%	US CORP BONDS 6.37%
US CORP BONDS 3.98%	SMALL CAP STOCKS -0.30%	FOREIGN STOCKS -43.38%	US CORP BONDS 12.79%	US GOV'T BONDS 9.37%	FOREIGN STOCKS -12.14%	NATURAL RESOURCES 2.20%	US CORP BONDS -2.38%	FOREIGN STOCKS -4.90%	EMERGING MARKET -14.92%	US GOV'T BONDS 1.35%
US GOV'T BONDS 2.67%	REAL ESTATE -18.15%	EMERGING MARKET -53.33%	US GOV'T BONDS -6.03%	FOREIGN STOCKS 7.75%	EMERGING MARKET -18.42%	US GOV'T BONDS 2.19%	EMERGING MARKET -2.60%	NATURAL RESOURCES -9.77%	NATURAL RESOURCES -24.28%	FOREIGN STOCKS 1.00%

Source: Callan Periodic Table of Investment Returns

In any given year, a diversified portfolio will never outperform the best-performing asset class or underperform the worst performing asset class. Rather, performance will be somewhere in between. Furthermore, no one is capable of consistently predicting which investments will shoot for the moon or hit rock bottom each year. Therefore, a diversified portfolio strategy attempts to integrate different asset classes and utilize how they interact with one another to increase overall returns with the least amount of risk. The key is to allow your diversified plan—rather than your emotions—dictate your investment strategy.

ENTER THE MODERN PORTFOLIO THEORY

The Modern Portfolio Theory is an investment approach that earned the 1990 Nobel Prize in Economics. It states that if you wish to increase the performance and reduce the risk in your investment portfolio, you should combine investments that are non-correlated with one another. Simply put, a truly diversified portfolio can provide the highest returns with the least amount of risk and volatility. In contrast, constructing a portfolio of investments that move in virtual lockstep with one another is one of the most dangerous things an investor can attempt.

You may be asking yourself, *How am I ever going to figure out how to invest in all of these asset classes myself?* Today, there's a pretty simple solution. It's called *target date funds.* These funds, which are offered by many companies, do the asset allocation for you. They manage the mix of stocks, bonds and all the asset classes. The breakdown all depends on the date you say you are going to enter your golden years. If you expect to retire in 2045, the fund will invest for you in a more aggressive stock-heavy portfolio. As you get older and closer to your retirement date, the fund will systematically reallocate to become less risky. It's a simple and effective approach to diversification.

Now that you're getting the idea about the importance of diversification among the asset classes, it's time to take it to the advanced class, which I call Diversification 2.0. I think you're going to like this, since it can mean significantly more money in your pockets and less in Uncle Sam's.

DIVERSIFICATION 2.0
CHANGING TIMES REQUIRE CHANGING STRATEGIES

The IRS sends out eight billion pages of forms and instructions each year. Laid end to end, they would stretch 28 times around the earth. I think it takes more of an effort to understand the income tax forms than it does to make the income we're taxed on. *The Washington Post* reports that 60 percent of taxpayers must hire a professional to get through their own return. Isn't it appropriate that the month taxes are due begins with April Fools' Day?

I've heard it said that America is a land of taxation that was founded to avoid taxation. Today, I believe that a truly diversified investment strategy must also take into consideration the impact of taxes. We've certainly concluded that diversification of investment allocations being spread out among various asset classes is imperative, and yet to truly get ahead in today's economic reality you need to diversify on the tax front as well. Which is exactly why I call this strategy, which is much easier to understand and implement than it may sound, Diversification 2.0.

Diversification 2.0 can provide you with the ability to minimize your tax liability in order to optimize the tax efficiency of your portfolio both today and in your future retirement years. Traditionally, individuals relied solely on their 401(k), IRAs or other tax-deferred vehicles for savings. I am a big fan of these accounts and use them myself. However, this one-dimensional savings strategy provides little to no flexibility when you eventually reach retirement. Diversification 2.0 involves spreading your investments among tax-deferred, tax-favored and taxable accounts during your working years to optimize your tax situation now as well as down the road. Below are the attributes to these different tax classifications.

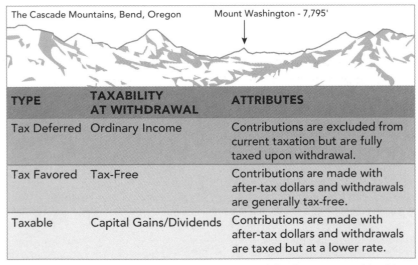

The Cascade Mountains, Bend, Oregon   Mount Washington - 7,795'

TYPE	TAXABILITY AT WITHDRAWAL	ATTRIBUTES
Tax Deferred	Ordinary Income	Contributions are excluded from current taxation but are fully taxed upon withdrawal.
Tax Favored	Tax-Free	Contributions are made with after-tax dollars and withdrawals are generally tax-free.
Taxable	Capital Gains/Dividends	Contributions are made with after-tax dollars and withdrawals are taxed but at a lower rate.

This case study is hypothetical in nature and does not provide legal, tax or accounting advice.

Would you like to cut your future tax bill in half? Stupid question. Of course you would! So does Alan, who has saved prudently for his retirement from the time he was in his mid 20s. Now it's finally time to retire and hopefully live the life he and his wife Judy have always imagined. Their goal is to live on an annual income stream of $100,000 from their investment portfolio.

Scenario 1: Oops, No Planning

Alan placed 100 percent of his savings in tax-deferred vehicles such as his IRA and 401(k). In his first year of retirement, he would be required to pay ordinary income tax on his entire distribution which, assuming current marginal tax brackets, would equal an estimated liability of $18,493.

	SOURCE OF FUNDS	TAX LIABILITY	TAX SAVINGS
NO PLANNING	100% Tax Deferred	$18,493	-
DIVERSIFICATION 2.0	50% Tax Deferred 25% Tax Favored 25% Taxable	$5,929 $0 $3,750	$8,814 (47.7%)

The Cascade Mountains, Bend, Oregon — Mount Jefferson -10,495'

This case study is based on 2013 marginal tax brackets, capital gains rates, standard deductions and exemptions.

Scenario 2: Diversification 2.0

Had Alan been introduced to the type of strategic investment planning I'm about to introduce you to during his accumulation years and used a combination of three different tax treatments, his tax liability would have been decreased by nearly 50 percent to $9,679 in his first year of retirement!

There will be a day when you start living off all the money you are saving. When you open the income valve to your 401(k), IRAs and other investment accounts, all the rules change. Not only are you no longer adding to your nest egg, you will need to make your money last for a possible 25 to 40 years. In retirement, you are faced with unique and potentially devastating risks as you begin the second half of your financial journey. Taxation is one of these risks. Diversification 2.0 can help you keep more of the money that you are working so hard for.

With proper diversification of the asset classes and tax classifications, your investments have a far greater chance of growing appropriately to provide you with a sound financial future. Remember, however, that it's also vital to keep our feelings in check, as both earning and losing money can be incredibly emotional. Research has shown time and time again that investors make major mistakes when they let their emotions rule. Whether you're climbing a mountain or investing for your financial future, you need to play it smart. That's next.

CHAPTER 6

PLAYING IT SMART

A smart man only believes half of what he hears.
A wise man knows which half.
—Jeff Cooper

As you may have figured out by now, I like living on the edge. To a point.

Shortly after moving to Bend in 2000, I joined a mountaineering club called the Cascades Mountaineers, where I started to meet new friends, most of whom I still keep in close contact with. This would prove to be the beginning of my Central Oregon adventures. In August of 2003, our group decided to climb Mount Washington, a peak with an elevation of 7,795 feet. This shield volcano is among the most recognized mountains in Oregon's Cascade Range, as it rises above the burned-over forest like nature's skyscraper.

Ironically, the fire I'm alluding to started the day we summited Mount Washington. The B&B Complex Fires eventually burned more than 90,000 acres over a period of five weeks. We watched the fire consume Douglas fir and Ponderosa pine with a vengeance, having no idea that the blaze would last for 34 days. At the peak of the firefighting effort, there were more than 2,300 personnel working on the blaze. The cost of fire suppression was more than $38 million. Days later, President George W. Bush would fly over the devastation after a Portland fundraising stop before heading down to play golf with his college buddies at Crosswater at Sunriver Resort. He was the first sitting president to visit Central Oregon. I remember thinking to myself, *Really, that's what it takes to get a president to Central Oregon.*

But I'm getting ahead of myself.

We accessed Mount Washington's slopes via the Pacific Crest Trail. Over the years, I'd been on several sections of this 1,100-mile stretch before reading *Wild,* Cheryl Strayed's journey of self-discovery. Fortunately, this trip would be a lot shorter than hers. Unfortunately, the rock on Mount Washington's steep slopes has a reputation for being extremely poor, reminiscent of a crumbling rock pile. Some feel it is not stable enough to climb. However, if you know what you're doing and are careful while doing it, there should be no problems.

Unlike most of the other nearby mountains—where you can hike and scramble to the summit in the summer months—all routes up Mount Washington are rated Class 5 or higher on the Yosemite Decimal System. Translation? Even though most climbers can easily reach the top without the aid of ropes, a fall can be fatal. So, we wisely opted for the protection of a rope to safely climb to the summit.

As we ascended, the hiking grew steeper, and the views more spectacular. Hot and sweaty, we eventually reached the summit block at 7,300 feet. The hike was over and the climb was beginning. Out came our helmets and harnesses. It was time to rope up. The first pitch is the chimney, a 60-foot wall of sharp and friable basalt. John Krog and Matt Gadow climbed ahead and set the rope, allowing Mark Daugherty and me to follow. All eyes were on the lookout for falling rock.

We reached the second pitch just below the summit, where I viewed Mount Jefferson and Three-Fingered Jack piercing through the thickening layer of smoke. The exposure was extreme, to say the least. I had originally started rock climbing to overcome my fear of heights. As we worked our way to the summit, I kept telling myself to look at the rock in front of me and not look below. I knew vertigo is all mental, and that I just needed to relax. So, I embraced the fact that after 50 feet it doesn't matter how high you are. If you fall, you're dead.

Before I knew it, our group of 11 was perched on the summit of Mount Washington, which could be a tabletop in heaven high above the world and, on this day, the mounting smoke below. For me, arriving at the summit of any awe-inspiring peak is a spiritual moment. Once I've been to the top, I never ever again seem to look at the mountain the same way.

Summiting Mount Washington – The Cascades Mountaineers and me
(helmet on chest)

It was now time for the second half of the journey. We prepared to leave the summit block and head to our rope. As
my climbing mentor, John Krog, always tells me, rappelling
down such a mountain begins with a test of trusting your
dear friend: *yourself*. Leaning back, you step off the edge with
rope in hand, feeding that rope through your ATC belay de-
vice, and begin the descent. The exposure below had my full
attention. To put it another way: *Gulp!*

For my climbing partners and me, it's essential to have the
right attitude and an adventurous spirit. You must trust your
partner, as well as inspecting and having confidence in your

gear. But most importantly, it's about not making foolish decisions. We all had the skill set to free climb the summit block without ropes. However, one slip, game over, and we'd be gone. *Double gulp!*

Just as we were playing things smart on the mountain by using ropes, you'll want to invest wisely so when you experience an oops you don't go into a financial free fall. Let's take a look at three all-too-common blunders so you don't make them yourself.

1. CHASING RETURNS — THE SMARTEST MAN IN THE WORLD

This story about a man who many regarded as the smartest man in the world should help you appreciate why chasing returns is never recommended.

Each year on December 31, this smartest man in the world would invest 100 percent of his investable assets into a single asset class, and each year his investment returns were stellar. Remember the Callan chart of asset classes bouncing around in the previous chapter? Year after year, this guy seemed to know the best-performing asset class to invest in. For example, in 2006 he knew to be 100 percent invested in real estate, that year's best-performing asset class. Then in 2008 he knew to switch to 100 percent U.S. treasuries, that year's best performer. An impossible skill that he had somehow mastered.

Each year at a family gathering on New Year's Day, he would tell his family all about his investment success and his brilliant investment clairvoyance. His brother-in-law, who had to endure this bragging about investment performance, decided he would try to replicate the Smartest Man's success by following his investment strategies. However, the brother-in-law was always a year behind the Smartest Man since he did not know what the strategy was until the following New Year. He assumed that if an investment did well in the prior year, it should be okay the following year. So when the Smartest Man was reallocating his portfolio into his next successful pick, the brother-in-law was chasing the previous return—investing into his old strategy.

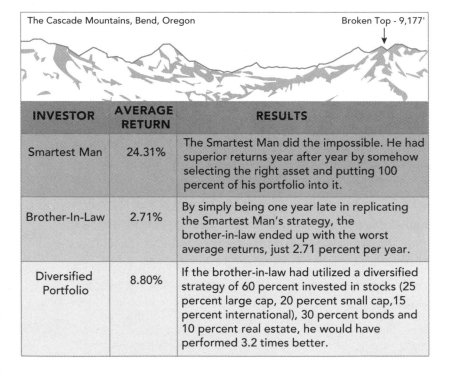

The Cascade Mountains, Bend, Oregon   Broken Top - 9,177'

INVESTOR	AVERAGE RETURN	RESULTS
Smartest Man	24.31%	The Smartest Man did the impossible. He had superior returns year after year by somehow selecting the right asset and putting 100 percent of his portfolio into it.
Brother-In-Law	2.71%	By simply being one year late in replicating the Smartest Man's strategy, the brother-in-law ended up with the worst average returns, just 2.71 percent per year.
Diversified Portfolio	8.80%	If the brother-in-law had utilized a diversified strategy of 60 percent invested in stocks (25 percent large cap, 20 percent small cap, 15 percent international), 30 percent bonds and 10 percent real estate, he would have performed 3.2 times better.

This went on for 10 years. Finally, in 2013, the brother-in-law decided to find out why he was not having the same success as the Smartest Man. On the previous page is a summary of his analysis between 2003 and 2012.

2. BUY LOW AND SELL HIGH

A study entitled "Quantitative Analysis of Investor Behavior" found that though the S&P 500 averaged an 11.8 percent return over a 20-year period, individuals failed much worse in their equity investments, averaging only a 4.5 percent annual return. How could this possibly be?

Anyone in business or real estate understands that to succeed you must buy low and sell high. And yet this is the exact opposite of what most investors do when they let their emotions rule. Investors typically look at the one-, three- and five-track records they receive from the investment company that manages their company 401(k) at the end of each year to see how the different investment options have performed. It is all too common to look at last year's winner with envy and think, *I want some of that!* So they invest, only to see that asset class sink the following year. By that time investors have lost confidence in that asset class. So what do they do? They sell it! To make matters worse, they typically buy it back when they have regained confidence in it once it's on top again. They are doing the exact opposite of what brings success. They are selling low and buying high.

Now you understand how some investors can easily fall victim to overemphasizing yesterday's winners, and how a diversified portfolio can help investors stay on track.

Warren Buffet, known as the greatest investor of our times, has a quote I enjoy sharing:

Be fearful when others are greedy, and be greedy when others are fearful.

His mantra may sound counterintuitive, but let's discuss it.

Before the crash in 2008, when many investors were purchasing real estate in hot markets such as Scottsdale, Miami, Las Vegas and even my hometown of Bend, Oregon, where it felt like prices were increasing in value on an hourly basis, Buffet would have passed. I'm sure he would have done the same with over-valued stocks. After the crash, however, when so many stockholders were trying to sell, he saw the challenging economy as an amazing opportunity. Back in 2008, Buffet wrote in a *New York Times* editorial:

Most certainly, fear is now widespread, gripping even seasoned investors. To be sure, investors are right to be wary of highly leveraged entities or businesses in weak competitive positions. But fears regarding the long-term prosperity of the nation's many sound companies make no sense. These businesses will indeed suffer earnings hiccups, as they always have. But most major companies will be setting new profit records 5, 10 and 20 years from now. Let me be clear on one point: I can't predict the short-term movements of the stock market. I haven't the faintest idea as to whether stocks will be higher or lower a month—or a year—from now. What is likely, however, is that the market will move higher, perhaps substantially so, well before either sentiment or the economy turns up. So, if you wait for the robins, spring will be over.

Nervous markets create opportunities, but as we've seen, you'll have to battle your emotions to keep your portfolio on course and stay committed to a long-term strategy. History shows that investments made in these moments of distress, when potential is much higher than normal, are usually the most rewarding.

I've said it before, but it bears repeating: Investing can be very emotional for investors. As a country, we have experienced record stock market growth over the past few years. Yet this also makes investors anxious as some wait for the next correction. *What should I do now?* they wonder. A more profitable question would be to ask, *How can I remove some of the unsettling feeling I have?*

My answer to the last question is to focus on a historical perspective, as it's all too common to focus on our current dilemmas without learning from the past.

Visualize a boy walking up a small mountain—or a butte, as we call them here in Central Oregon—with a yoyo in his hand. His rising and falling yoyo symbolizes the economy, real estate or stock market. As the yoyo goes up, we tend to experience exuberance. As it falls, feelings of anxiety can creep in. As the yoyo starts its next ascent, we celebrate with enthusiasm. And then before we know it, gravity takes over and the yoyo faces a downward spiral and our stomachs begin to feel queasy as apprehension sets in once again. Each of us can decide whether to focus on the rising and falling yoyo or the boy. You see, they both reach the top with its majestic vistas at the exact same time.

What will you focus on?

Wayne Gretzky's advice says it all:

I skate to where the puck is going to be, not to where it has been.

Let's look at another fatal mistake too many investors continue to make.

3. IT IS TIME IN THE MARKETS — NOT TIMING THE MARKETS!

The word *recession* has become taboo for our society over time. What most people don't realize is that our economy averages a recession every nine years. This is, and always has been, our reality. By taking this historical perspective and realizing that there has never been a down real estate or stock market that has not bounced back to hit an all-time high, it becomes that much easier to emotionally overcome the inevitable challenging markets that will always poke their heads out.

Mark Twain brought some comic relief to such a topic when he said;

> October: This is one of the particularly dangerous months to invest in stocks. Other dangerous months are July, January, September, April, November, May, March, June, December, August and February.

A few years back, I was introduced to a new client who shared his perceived success story. In an excited tone, he explained that he had liquidated his entire equity portfolio in October 2007 when the DJIA was near its peak closing price at that time of 14,164. He went on to give details about how the Dow hit a market low of 6,443 on March 6, 2009, having lost more than 54 percent of its value since the October 2007 high.

I asked him when he had gotten back in the market. He said in a much less enthusiastic tone that he had not done that yet; he was waiting for the markets to decline before investing. I informed him that the markets had since experienced momentous growth and the Dow had more than doubled, achieving a new all-time high. I didn't have to add that he had lost out. By the time I was done, he knew. As I have already shared with you, by 2017 the markets were up more than 300 percent from 2009.

When you time the markets, you have to be lucky twice. You must not only get out of the markets at the right time, you need to get back in at the right time. This gentleman had been lucky once but not twice, and consequently now faces the serious dilemma of not having enough money for his retirement, a situation I hope you never find yourself in.

The evidence has shown that market timing just doesn't work. With that in mind, here are some additional thoughts on this topic from some of the brightest minds in the industry:

💰 Peter Lynch is considered a legend in the financial media for his management of Fidelity Investment's Magellan Fund:

Far more money has been lost by investors preparing for corrections, or trying to anticipate corrections, than has been lost in corrections themselves. I can't recall ever once having seen the name of a market timer on Forbes' annual list of the richest people in the world. If it were truly possible to predict corrections, you'd think somebody would have made billions by doing it.

💰 Benjamin Graham, the Columbia Business School economist who is known as Warren Buffet's investment mentor:

In the financial markets, hindsight is forever 20/20, but foresight is legally blind. And thus, for most investors, market timing is a practical and emotional impossibility.

💰 Warren Buffet:

My favorite time frame is forever. The only value of stock forecasters is to make fortune-tellers look good.

💰 *Fortune* magazine:

Let's say it clearly: No one knows where the market is going—experts or novices, soothsayers or astrologers. That's the simple truth.

💰 *The Wall Street Journal:*

A decade of results throws cold water on the notion that strategists exhibit any special ability to time the markets.

Instead of fighting an exhausting battle with your emotions, develop a diversified long-term strategy and stick to it. After all, your long-term goals don't change overnight, so why should your portfolio?

We have seen how investors make some pretty serious mistakes. We have all made mistakes in our lives, and I'm sure we'll continue to do so. But nothing may top the dim-witted mistake I made on my first ever ocean scuba dive. I'll share that one next as a way of helping you to protect yourself on the financial front.

CHAPTER 7

YOUR 0 GUIDE TO FINANCIAL SURVIVAL

Everyone is entitled to be stupid,
but some abuse the privilege.

M y survival instinct wasn't always as strong as it is today.

Ever since I watched *The Undersea World of Jacques Cousteau* TV shows as a child, I've wanted to join him in the depths of the sea with a self-contained underwater breathing apparatus. Yes, that's where the word scuba comes from. Diving seemed like the coolest activity under the sun. I was 17 years old and the concept of hanging out below with the vibrant fish and coral seemed surreal. I decided I would become a certified diver. Living in the mountains of Upstate New York, nowhere near the ocean beaches, my instruction took place in a community swimming pool. After a few months of both weekly classroom lessons and practical (in-pool) sessions,

I thankfully passed the written exam. My final checkout dive took place in ice-cold Lake George—to this date my favorite lake on the entire planet. I became a proud card-carrying member of PADI, the agency that dominates worldwide scuba certification. I was thrilled. This permitted me to dive anywhere in the world and I wanted to see it all.

With an affinity for jumping in headfirst, I immediately subscribed to Scuba Diving magazine and purchased a pre-owned Scubapro buoyancy compensator and regulator, a Sherwood air tank, along with the obligatory weight belt, mask, fins, snorkel and dive knife. My new black wet suit had a bright red stripe down the sides with a customary tight fit that I felt gave me a momentarily buff physique.

My cousin Jon, a few years my senior, was an experienced diver. After learning about my recent training, he invited me to join him on a dive trip to Catalina Island. Previously owned by the chewing gum magnate William Wrigley, Jr., whose family generously donated a majority of the 76 square miles of this priceless earth to the Catalina Island Conservancy in 1975, the arid, mountainous island is located just 22 miles off the coast of Southern California.

As the high-speed catamaran carrying several hundred passengers entered the harbor in the charming, picturesque town of Avalon, with the exclusive yachts lining the waterfront, I imagined I was in Dubrovnik, Croatia or Monaco. We disembarked. I breathed in the salty air and felt that all was right with the world. Unfortunately, this peaceful, easy feeling immediately shifted to anxiety the moment Jon informed me that we would be diving that very evening.

"What do you mean diving this evening?" I asked.

"There is nothing better than night diving! The colors are much more vivid than they are during the day when the sunlight gets absorbed. On a night dive, your light source is never more than five or 10 feet away, so the water doesn't take away any of the light spectrum. We'll wind up seeing unexpected surprises as well as great beauty."

"That's great, Jon," I said in a sarcastic tone. "But this is my first time diving in the ocean. I am familiar with chlorine, not salt water. I'm not searching for unexpected surprises yet. I've never even used underwater lights. This is all new to me!"

I would have been happy to meet in the middle by starting my diving career at dusk when I would have the convenience of gearing up while it was relatively light, but still get the effect of making a night dive. Nope, Jon was fixated on showing me the bioluminescence, where divers can wave their hands in front of their faces and watch the sparks fly. The light show is caused by the biochemical emission of light by tiny organisms—phytoplankton—in the water. Do you think I cared about this? Not one bit. My excitement for diving was quickly turning into terror. Sure, I was very comfortable swimming in deep mountain lakes and flowing rivers, but the ocean was a different beast with animal life that could eat you! To say I was apprehensive before stepping into the dark void of an unlit ocean is another massive understatement.

Jon Rappaport and me, scuba diving at Catalina Island

The dive—my first, let's not forget—would have been disconcerting in the best of circumstances. Maneuvering with fins and an air tank is a cumbersome undertaking when not in the water and I felt about as graceful as a hippopotamus on ice skates. I had to catch my breath as the chilly water sent down directly from the Alaskan currents entered my wet suit. Before long my body heat would warm the trapped water inside, but until then the shrinkage factor would have made Jerry Seinfeld proud. All 125 lumens from our TUSA dive lights lit the way as we awkwardly entered the mysterious waters from the rocky shore beneath the Catalina Casino, the island's most historic landmark.

Jon had shared with me how night diving might be the clos-est thing to experiencing blindness, as everything is pitch dark except for the limited area directly in front of your light. Peripheral vision is nonexistent. I would soon learn that he was not exaggerating. We quickly reviewed the international diving hand signals so we would be speaking a similar lan-guage once under. You can probably imagine the hand signal I really wanted to bestow on him.

If there's one aspect of night diving that is more complicat-ed than day diving, it's communication. We would need to shine our light directly on our hands in order to see what signal the other was using. I clung to my light like a security blanket. We floated out until we were well past our capabil-ity to stand. It was time to place our masks over our fac-es and salty regulators into our mouths. I looked at Jon, my eyes bulging, and submerged into the mysterious waters. It became immediately evident that giant kelp thrives in cold, clear, nutrient-rich waters. The sinister seaweed engulfed us like a family of octopus. I later learned we were in a kelp for-est. I had never heard of such a thing. I stayed close to Jon, as it is very easy to become separated from your buddy in this dense environment.

I could see nothing. No matter how wide I opened my eyes, I was looking into a void. I scanned my handheld light back and forth, looking for something. Anything. I found it all right. Looking directly into my eyes, just inches away, was a monstrous, prehistoric creature equipped with never-end-ing sharp teeth. Holy crap, Batman! I wonder if the caped crusader ever warmed up his suit the way I almost warmed up mine. This six-foot-long, one-foot-in-diameter green creature looked downright evil. I had never even heard of a green moray eel, but it is easy to see why they are often feared and mistaken for sea serpents. Their vicious reputation may come from the fact that they continually open and close their mouths to take in water in order to breathe, showing off a set of chompers that could easily tear into a stack of New York deli corned beef sandwiches piled one on top of the other.

Green Moray Eel - Gymnothorax funebris

I darted for the surface at an alarming rate that should have required emergency transport to a hyperbaric chamber. Rule

#1 in scuba is to never dive without a dive buddy. Rule #2 is to never ascend at a faster rate than the bubbles created by your regulator. It took me less than a minute to breach the surface. Bad news.

My heart was nearly jumping out of my 6mm polypropylene suit. I felt lucky to be alive. I had no idea how lucky I really was. When you come up too fast from a dive, you can experience decompression sickness, commonly called the bends, which is extremely painful and can even be fatal. That's why divers take courses to receive deep-water dive certification, training that includes a thorough understanding of the risks and safety procedures for descending and ascending to avoid the hazards associated with changes in pressure. But I was in such a state of distress and shock that my lack of experience and innate instincts had overridden my recent training.

Looking back, we were stupid, stupid, stupid. There are some things you just don't do on your first ocean dive, and night diving in a kelp forest are two of them. Diving at a site that you have not experienced during daylight is a third, and the list goes on. I should not have been there. I was a diving novice whose knowledge about diving was sketchy at best.

So, here's the question. Are you being stupid when it comes to money?

SINK OR SWIM

Many intelligent people are inexperienced when it comes to investing and would consider themselves financially illiterate. If you feel like you fall into this category, let me tell you, you are certainly not alone. Why is this? It may be due to the fact that our schools are not teaching the simple financial basics, including personal finance. Can you imagine if you had learned about compound interest and the doubling of a penny in your childhood? Unfortunately, a Macroeconomics 101 course just doesn't do the job of preparing you for your financial future. It is time for our schools to bear some of the responsibility for teaching these ever-so-important financial lessons.

I also believe that we are hardwired to make financial mistakes because most of our financial lessons have come from our parents. When it comes right down to it, what do most of them know about personal finance?

The other major source of financial education comes from the constant barrage of so-called authorities on 24-hour television news. These financial pundits are well aware that fear and pessimism sells, and their primary objective seems to be increasing their Nielsen ratings. With headlines that highlight words like *panic* and *collapse*, today's economic news could be considered financial pornography.

We need to overcome both this lack of education and our reaction to the media's fearmongering by getting smarter when it comes to money. Pete Seeger said:

Education is when you read the fine print. Experience is what you get if you don't.

I want to help ensure you don't make terrible decisions like I did on Catalina Island. So instead of plunging into a financial abyss that's even scarier than unknown creatures in a dark underwater kelp forest, let's discuss some concerns as well as some ideas to increase your financial security and the amount of money you have to save and invest each month. I'll also divulge eight common blunders I see young investors making with their 401(k)s, so you don't follow suit.

All too often, financial advice focuses on investing. But you can't invest if you are spending every dime you make. How much money you save is far more important than how much money you earn. In other words, as I've said before, it's not what you make, it's what you keep.

Which person do you think will have a brighter financial future? The all-too-common scenario of a person who earns $100,000 a year and spends $110,000, or the person who earns $50,000 and lives on only 90 percent of this income, investing $5,000 for the future?

If you don't want to face the financial equivalent of a bunch of moray eels, here are some straightforward steps to bring your financial planning to life:

✓   Spend less than you earn.
✓   Save what you do not spend.
✓   Invest what you save.

WHERE DID IT GO?

Many people earn just enough money to make ends meet, yet often they do not have a clear picture of where their money actually goes. When I hear someone explain such typical circumstances, I'll often ask them when they last visited a coffee shop. Their typical answer is: *On my way to work this morning.*

I had an opportunity to meet fellow financial author, David Bach, when he spoke in Bend a number of years ago. In his book *Finish Rich*, he coined a now well-known phrase: *the latte factor*. The phrase comes from the notion that if you added up the cost of your daily lattes or other similar drinks and saved or invested that money, you could create significant prosperity over time and certainly over a much shorter time frame. The trivial things we spend money on every day add up to a considerable amount of money over time. Most people are unaware of how much they spend on the little stuff each day.

You'll probably agree with me that it's very easy to spend $10 a day on inconsequential purchases. Let's take a look at the simple math. If you were to save and invest this $10 a day or $300 a month into an investment that yielded a conservative 6 percent return, over the course of 20 years you will have accumulated over $142,000. Over 40 years this amount surges to almost $600,000! This can certainly help add perspective.

I recently returned from a speaking engagement in beautiful Chicago. I stayed at the Palmer House, one of Chicago's grandest hotels, dating back to 1873. In the lobby was a nationally known coffee shop. Each morning the line for caffeine would go all the way around the corner. I was amazed how much of a premium they were able to demand due to their convenient location. This reminded me of a story that Darren Hardy, the editor of *Success Magazine*, tells.

To paraphrase him, he says there are three different types of people. If you could hear the way each thought while in line to purchase coffee, you would immediately be able to determine if they were destined to achieve financial independence in their life or be destined to a life of financial mediocrity.

The first group would ask themselves if they wanted to have a cup of coffee. If the answer was yes, they would then ask themselves, *What do I have to do to get the coffee?* Governed by impulses and emotions, they might beg, borrow or even steal to satisfy their need for caffeine, sugar or any other immediately gratified desire.

I believe most people fall into the second group. This crowd would ask themselves. *Do I have $5 to purchase a cup of specialty coffee?* This may sound perfectly reasonable, but this is why most people are of average means. This group is certainly more fiscally responsible than the first group, as they will only spend money they have. However, their focus is on the here and now; they are not contemplating how such a simple decision could negatively impact their entire financial future.

I find that the people who have achieved financial independence on their own think in a way that is quite different from the rest of the herd. This third group would reflect on the same coffee scenario and ask themselves a very different question. *If I invest this $5 rather than spend it on this cup of coffee, what could this money grow to over time?*

Well, let's take a look—$5 growing at 8 percent over 30 years would accumulate to over $50. This is 10 times the original amount! They would then ask themselves, *Is this $5 coffee worth $50 to me?* While in the accumulation phase of their lives, this unique group of people would choose to pass on the coffee today in order to achieve true financial freedom later.

I have to admit that I get joy from buying myself an Americano at local coffee shops. I just love the combination of their delicious blends, friendly service and enjoyable atmosphere in which to meet friends and colleagues. However, I have made the conscious decision to make this a treat in my life and not a daily habit.

I greatly admire how the wise and inspiring third group of people thinks in a different way. Here are some of the life and financial principles I observe them living by:

✓ The tougher you are on yourself today, the easier life will be later. (I know, I've said it before. But it's an important point.)

✓ Rather than always working for money, make your money work for you by living below your means and investing the difference for your future.

✓ You don't need to do anything extraordinary to accumulate wealth. You just need to do some ordinary
things extraordinarily well. Living on 90 percent of
your paycheck rather than on more than 100 percent
is a great start.

✓ There's power in compound interest.

If you incorporate these principles into your life, I believe you
can have the financial freedom to not only make a specialty
coffee part of your daily life in the future, but to experience
an espresso in places like Venice, Barcelona, Amsterdam or
wherever your heart desires.

A comfortable financial future starts with saving now. One
step is to track your expenses so you know where your money is actually going. We'll chat more about that in the next
chapter when we discuss budgeting. Another step involves
putting those oh-so-accessible debit and credit cards on ice.

FREEZE THE PLASTIC

James W. Frick said:

> Don't tell me where your priorities are. Show me where
> you spent your money and I'll tell you what they are.

Despite relatively high incomes compared to the rest of the
world, most Americans have a challenging time saving their
money for one major reason. We have become professional
consumers, often spending more than we can ever afford.

Thanks to credit and debit cards along with ATM machines on every corner, your money is available for spending 24 hours a day. Credit for individuals is easily available again, and this is where the danger begins. Oh, how effortless it is to rack up high-interest charges on purchases you often can't afford in the first place. This not only wreaks havoc with your personal finances, it delays your progress toward achieving your financial goals in your soon-to-be-created financial plan. When is the last time you heard someone say they had decided to forgo a purchase because they were saving for a future home or a time when they may work because that is what they choose to do, not because they are dependent on a paycheck?

Each year, consumers pay millions of dollars in interest on consumer debts such as credit cards, student loans and auto loans. Debt is a problem that does not age well. It's time to get serious about paying off debt. Let's say you have a credit card with a 15 percent annual percentage rate (APR) and close to a $16,000 balance, the average for Americans. This equates to monthly interest payments of about $200. If you don't pay it off, over a period of a year, those credit card purchases you made will cost you an extra $2,400. If it takes you five years to pay off that credit card debt, you'll have spent an extra $12,000. Those deals you scored are suddenly not looking that great, are they?

Even if you're intent on saving money, paying off debt could be a smart move given the interest rate on debt versus the rate one may currently earn from saving. So let's say you have stacked up $5,000 on your credit card, have $25,000 remaining on your student loan debt, and have a mortgage and a car loan. Which should you pay off first? In almost all scenarios, the interest on your credit card will be significantly higher than the rest and this debt should be eliminated first, even though it has the lower balance. Also, keep in mind that your mortgage interest is tax-deductible.

Setting up automatic recurring monthly payments is an effective way to attack your debt rather than hoping there's some extra at the end of the month. We all know how those unexpected spending opportunities can pop up at a moment's notice. This is why paying down your debt at the beginning of each month, even if your minimum payment isn't due until later in the month, is prudent. You'll feel energized as you see your debt start to decrease month after month.

PREPARE FOR THAT RAINY DAY

The best way to stay out of debt is to create a fund to protect yourself from the unknown. While the last decade's recession may already be a fading memory, many Americans are just one unexpected bill away from financial disaster. A recent survey from Bankrate.com shows that a majority of Americans (63 percent) may not have enough money in their savings to cover an unexpected $1,000 hospital emergency room visit or a $500 car repair. While it's commendable to pay down your debt as swiftly as possible, it's also important to pay yourself a little something into a savings account each month. Even minimal amounts deposited from each paycheck can provide an admirable rainy-day account over time.

Living paycheck to paycheck is not the way anyone wants to live. But since you're reading this book, you clearly already know that, which puts the financial odds in your favor.

Here's another tip. When most people think *savings,* they think about placing it in a bank. However, this has its own risks due to the damaging impact of inflation (more about that later). Money that's earmarked for your long-term future ought to be invested into one of the qualified retirement accounts, such as a 401(k), that we learned about in Chapter 3.

THE ABCs OF 401(k)s

While 401(k)s are a killer investment opportunity for those of you lucky enough to work for an employer who offers them, far too often I see investors making a number of bad choices when it comes to these ever-so-popular investment homes. Let's look at the eight biggest mistakes so that you don't follow suit.

1. Owning Too Much of Your Company Stock

There are no guarantees of how much you'll have in your 401(k) by retirement. The amount you end up with depends on two factors: how much you contribute while working and what growth your money experiences based on the investments you choose.

If shares of your own company's stock are an investment choice in your 401(k), you may want to consider restricting your allocation to no more than 10 percent. This does not mean you are disloyal. I often see employees investing too much of their money in their employer's stock. Sadly, this happened to a friend of mine back in 2001. She worked for Enron, at the time one of the country's largest energy companies. Even though she had numerous investment options inside of her 401(k) retirement plan, she chose to invest 100 percent of her 401(k) in her company's stock, as she wanted to share in the significant growth it had been experiencing. In June of 2000, Enron stock hit an all-time high, selling for over $90 per share. By October of the following year, Enron was part of the largest bankruptcy in American history up to that point in time, plummeting to under $1 per share. She lost everything she had saved in her 401(k) retirement plan. Had she diversified her investments among all the asset classes and purchased only a portion of Enron stock, she would have mitigated the risk and her portfolio would be providing her with significant retirement income today. There are plenty of other colossal companies that have vanished over the years—think Kodak, Washington Mutual, WorldCom, Blockbuster and Borders, to name a few. Repeat after me: Diversify, diversify, diversify.

2. Leaving Money on the Table
According to a recent study conducted by the Financial Industries Regulatory Authority (FINRA), almost 30 percent of American workers do not contribute enough to their 401(k) retirement plans to receive their employer's matching contribution. It is estimated that every year, billions of investment dollars are left on the table by employees who just don't take advantage of this no-brainer action. Let me remind you:

💰 It is typical for employers to match dollar for dollar the first 3 percent or more of their employees' income in 401(k) retirement plans. If your employer offers such a program and you're not already taking full advantage of it, you are basically throwing away free money. For example, if you earn $50,000 per year before taxes, your employer will match the first $1,500 (3 percent of $50,000) that you contribute to your retirement plan. By the end of the year, you will have accumulated $3,000 for your financial future. This is made up of the $1,500 you had deducted from your paycheck along with the free match of $1,500 that your employer contributed into *your* account. This does not even factor in any potential gains your account may have received for the year. There is nowhere else I have ever seen where you can get a 100 percent rate of return. Guaranteed! That's $1,500 of free money. Why would you turn down free money?

💰 If you were to contribute $1,500 per year, your actual out-of-pocket cost wouldn't even be that amount. Here's why. Any money you contribute to a 401(k) reduces your taxable income. If you're earning $50,000 and you're a single filer, you're in the 25 percent tax bracket. That means your taxable income will be reduced by $1,500 and you would save $375 ($1,500 x 25 percent = $375) in taxes, so your actual out-of-pocket investment cost is $1,125, or $94 per month.

$ When you sign up to contribute to the retirement plan your company offers, your employer will usually systematically deduct the amount you request from each paycheck. I call this paying yourself first. After a month or two, you will barely notice the difference in your paychecks. However, you'll be amazed how such an ordinary task will yield such extraordinary results for you over time. As the years pass, you'll have socked away a considerable sum for your financial future.

Don't walk away from this incomparable opportunity to begin or increase funding your company's 401(k) or whatever retirement plan they offer.

3. Considering Your 401(k) as a Glorified Savings Account

Many 401(k) plans also allow employees to take loans from their 401(k), which means that you can access a portion of your own retirement plan money if needed before retirement. Technically these loans are not true loans because they do not involve a lender or an assessment of your credit score and you will be paying back the principal and interest on the loan to yourself, not to some bank or other financial institution. Additionally, this type of loan is not taxable income or subject to the 10 percent early withdrawal penalty as long as it's paid back in accordance with the IRS guidelines. Those guidelines require you to repay the money you have accessed within five years to restore your 401(k) plan to approximately its original state, as though the transaction never occurred.

While this may seem advantageous due to the often-reasonable interest rates and the fact that you are paying the interest back into your own account, I suggest only taking advantage of this opportunity in an emergency rather than using your retirement account as a glorified ATM to purchase that new 65-inch Quantum Dot Color curved-screen TV. On the other hand, using the money to help you purchase your first primary residence could make sense. But that's the exception rather than the rule. Here are some important reasons why I don't usually recommend taking a loan from your 401(k).

💰 If you don't pay it back over time, you will have to pay taxes on the money you took out at your current tax rate plus an additional 10 percent penalty if you took it out before age 59½.

💰 If you lose or change your job, you will need to repay the entire loan in full within a short period, usually within 30 to 60 days, which most people can't do after the loss of a job or while in transition. If you can't, the IRS considers the money you've loaned yourself to be a withdrawal, which means you'll have to pay taxes at your current rate. As we just saw, if you're under age 59½, you will experience that 10 percent penalty as well.

💰 The dollars you borrowed are losing the benefits of investment growth and aren't compounding for your future. This could leave you with smaller savings, as you're losing out on the future value of those borrowed funds.

💰 If you stop making additional contributions while you are paying back your loan, you won't receive any employer matching contributions.

By borrowing from your 401(k), you're defeating the purpose of this tax-advantaged savings opportunity. Unless you need the money for an emergency or possibly your first home, let it ride and rise for the exciting life you have ahead of you.

4. Liquidating Your 401(k) Account When You Switch Jobs
When you leave your employer, you have the option to liquidate the investments inside your 401(k) plan. This may feel like a great departing bonus or severance at the time, and such a large chunk of change may provide you with that new car or trip that has been calling your name. Once again, you need to understand the consequences. Uncle Sam will be hitting you with some major taxes come April 15th, as well as that frustrating 10 percent penalty if you're under the age of 59½. This can potentially sabotage your quest for financial freedom.

To keep the funds working for your future, it's beneficial to rollover the 401(k) plan from your previous employer to the 401(k) plan with your new employer. Although you can usually leave your 401(k) plan with the old employer intact, not doing so will simplify your life in the following ways.

💰 Consolidating your two or more retirement accounts will enable them to grow together.

💰 It will be much easier to keep track of your investments when they are all in one place, and to make sure that your holdings are diversified and that you don't have too many eggs in a single basket.

💰 You will receive only one quarterly statement and one annual prospectus explaining the guidelines rather than numerous ones. This will also save our trees!

💰 You can cleanly break all ties with your past employer and not have to contact that company's HR department every time you have questions or requests.

💰 Electing a rollover to the new plan does not subject you to any income tax or early withdrawal penalties, and keeps the money working for your future.

Although this is uncommon, if your new employer's plan does not permit rollovers or you do not like the fund options in the new 401(k) plan account, you can also choose to rollover your old account balance into a traditional IRA where you can have access to a broader array of investment choices. You may also want to consider converting these dollars to a Roth IRA, which I discussed in Chapter 3.

5. Failing to Rebalance Your 401(k)

It is all too common to see new investors put time and energy into choosing an array of diversified investments inside of their 401(k), then let the funds ride over extended periods of time to the point where they become out of balance. In a really good year, the more precarious growth stock portion of your portfolio may grow exponentially. You can best preserve that growth by rebalancing it to an allocation that will enable you to continue to grow your retirement savings without taking on unnecessary risk. I suggest meeting with your company's plan administrator each year to review your current allocations and portfolio choices.

While failing to rebalance your portfolio can jeopardize your retirement savings, so can playing it too safe. So you don't want to go to the other extreme of shying away from risk altogether.

6. Avoiding Risk Completely

Many investors who do not feel confident in their ability to invest intelligently seem to steer clear of risk completely. At least that's the intent. So they place their money in what they consider safe investments. These often include CDs, the money market or other guaranteed savings options. The predicament is that these investments usually do not keep pace with the inflation rate that averages between 3 and 4 percent each year. While they may see their account value increase slightly on an annual basis, they are actually losing purchasing power. One guideline I have heard over the years is to subtract your age from 110. The answer you get is the percentage of money you may want to allocate to stocks. For example, if you are 35 years old, then 75 percent of your portfolio should be invested into stocks (110 - 35 = 75).

7. Not Increasing Your Savings When Your Income Increases

Just because you started to save for your financial future by simply enrolling in a 401(k) doesn't necessarily mean you are saving enough. But that's an easy thing to ignore. All too often, when people receive a 5 percent raise, they increase their standard of living by 7 percent rather than maintaining their level of comfort and increasing their 401(k) or IRA contributions. If your goal is to replace a similar portion of your current income during your years of retirement, it's important that you increase the amount you put aside based on the amount you earn. So celebrate your next raise and all the raises that follow by increasing your retirement account contributions each time.

8. The Biggest Mistake of All: Doing Nothing or Waiting Too Long to Start

I do not want to disparage the pressure so many millennials are currently experiencing with student loan debts that average almost $30,000. If that sounds like the mountain you have to climb, you're not alone. *U.S. News & World Report* states an estimated 40 million Americans carry student loans and about 70 percent of today's students graduate college with debt.

With these statistics, it's no surprise that saving for your future often takes a back seat. In addition, millennials are an underemployed generation, which makes the situation even more hair-raising. I know it's incredibly challenging, but I am here to both share a blinding flash of the obvious and try to motivate you to keep telling yourself, *The tougher you are on yourself today, the easier life will be on you later!*

We were all born to procrastinate. That's why there are deadlines and extensions. Unfortunately, deadlines and extensions don't exist when it comes to your financial future. It's happening right now. Zig Ziglar said it best:

> *If you can't take a huge step to begin with, take as big a step as you can but take it now!*

Along the same vein, he also said:

> *When you discipline yourself to do the things you need to do when you need to do them, the day is going to come when you get to do the things you want when you want to do them.*

It's so discouraging that most people spend more time planning their adventurous getaways than they do their finances—and by now you know how much I love my adventures. If you spend more time planning your finances now, you will have a great many more vacations and overseas adventures to plan in your future. Does that sound appealing? Now is the time to take charge of your finances! To add a little humor to a serious topic, it's been said that doing nothing is hard because you just never know when you're done. And that's no way to live a life.

So, start saving as early as you can. The most important asset you have when saving for retirement is time. The earlier you start saving, the easier it will be to achieve your financial goals. Here's another startling fact to help motivate you: Every six years you wait to get started doubles the required monthly savings necessary to reach the same level of retirement income. As fellow author and speaker Michael Hyatt says: *When would NOW be a good time to do it?* I suggest you review the IRA chart on page 38 that Grandma Ruth shared with me. Then start saving now and *keep climbing.*

By avoiding the money mistakes listed above, you'll set yourself up for a far greater chance of success. And here's the most important thing to remember when it comes to achieving your financial goals: *If you fail to plan, you are planning to fail.* To help you navigate both your dollars and sense, it is imperative to have a plan.

CHAPTER 8

"CUZ IF YOU DON'T HAVE A PLAN, THEN TELL ME WHAT YOU GOT"

*Someone's sitting in the shade today because someone
planted a tree a long time ago.*
—Warren Buffett

It was 1994 and my plan was to complete the second half
of my journey through Africa. Memories of getting stuck
on safari in Kenya already felt like a lifetime ago. Next stop:
the former Republic of Rhodesia, currently named Zimbabwe. This landlocked nation was just beginning to enjoy the
economic benefits of tourism. While I was looking forward
to experiencing the country's natural beauty, the challenge
before me was a somber one. To get to Harare, Zimbabwe's
capital city, I would need to cross through Mozambique,
which until recently had been experiencing a civil war that
had begun in 1977.

Mozambique's civil war pitted FRELIMO, the socialist-styled government that backed the anti-apartheid efforts of the African National Congress in South Africa, against RENAMO, led by Western-styled rebels, many of whom were mercenaries paid by the white governments of South Africa and the former Rhodesia. Their mission: to disrupt a black African-led FRELIMO, and consequently Mozambique.

To get through this war-torn area, I would need to drive several hours through the Tete Corridor, infamously known as the Gun Run. Appallingly, an estimated one million people died there and five million civilians, many of whom were made amputees by landmines, were displaced. Although Zimbabwe was holding the country's first multi-party elections since the war had officially ended three years earlier in 1992, the area was anything but secure. I was warned to be vigilant, as carjacking, assault and robbery were known to be commonplace. Sadly, I knew from experience to fear even more the police and border control—young men with their AK-47s.

My heart felt like it was going burst out of my chest and my palms were slippery with sweat when the bus I was traveling on was randomly stopped at a patrol station. Would this be another "document check" with the intention of soliciting bribes? Most African people's smiles extend all the way to their eyes, but these uniformed men only shared unyielding glares.

As the only Mzungu aboard the half-empty bus, I was nervous that I would be picked out. The young men with the semi-automatic weapons asked us to remove our luggage from the bus before waiting in a line to complete their bureaucratic forms. I felt totally out of control, as I did during most of my African adventure. The only thing that reassured me was that I had stashed small denominations of the local currency in a pocket as well as in my shoes and my backpack, which I could hand over if asked, rather than expose the money belt that lined my abdomen under my shirt.

Finally, they let us go. Relief does not begin to describe how I felt when my backpack—my sustenance and shelter—and I were given authorization to get back on the bus. A few hours later I made it unscathed across this 300-kilometer corridor.

I spent the next two days exploring the more modern city of Harare. This would be the first time in months I would see familiar sights from back home, including fast-food restaurants, department stores, traffic lights, super markets and cinemas. It was also the first time I experienced Africa's white residents, whose BMWs were washed by black servants living in shantytown houses made of cardboard and corrugated metal. After months in the African countryside, it was all a bit overwhelming. It also made me feel angry to experience this inequality first hand.

I wanted to visit Chimanimani National Park, probably Africa's least-known nature reserve, and made it to the small village of Chimanimani after hitching a ride from a local farmer. I was happy to meet Moira from North England at the simple yet cozy lodge called Heaven. She was also traveling solo and looking to spend a few days in the park. Years later, as the father of a teenage daughter, it feels daunting to contemplate a young woman traveling unaccompanied through Africa. At the time, I was just pleased to have stumbled upon a companion.

Hiking through Chimanimani National Park, Zimbabwe, Africa

We stocked up on the essentials. Once our provisions were carefully positioned in our backpacks, we set off for the ranger station where we signed in and obtained detailed maps of the park. The path went vertical right from the start and the climb suddenly felt serious. We passed rocky barricades and eventually reached a high grassy plateau with a moon-like landscape of enormous boulders the size of houses randomly spread around. From here the jagged, crystalline Chimanimani Mountains were front and center, forming the border with Mozambique.

This park is a hikers' paradise of pristine wilderness, wild and unspoiled. There are no roads, only narrow footpaths. It's certainly not Yosemite. You do not come here to drive around the park or follow meandering roads through the valley. Here you need good hiking boots, strong legs and a lust for the great outdoors.

The valley is riddled with hundreds of small caves and overhangs ideal for camping. We set our sights on the Red Wall Cave known for its spectacular views and its proximity to the adjacent Bundi River. By early evening, map in hand, tired and hungry, we arrived. The cave was perfect, a cozy, warm opening in the enormous iron-imbedded rock wall with a bed of dried grass. The campfire provided us with a hot rice-and-bean soup meal and illuminated the rock ceiling. As the Southern Cross began to glow in the night sky, contented sighs filled our shelter.

The next day we needed to recover from our 12-mile hike to the cave. After a slow start, we headed off to spend the day at a few of the numerous streams and pools scattered throughout the park. It was the perfect way to beat the afternoon heat. We eventually found Digby's waterfall, hands down the most scenic oasis I had ever seen. After a swim to both clean up and cool off in the frigid mountain water, I napped on a warm rock. The afternoon heat became intense and there was no shade in sight. Moira turned her sarong into a canopy with a few sticks. Time slipped into the future as our watches read 4:30 p.m.

Red Wall Cave painting from my journal

Eventually we realized we had to leave our little paradise and began to slowly work our way back up the path to our cave to make dinner. We knew we had a 40-minute hike ahead of us and that the hot days here quickly turn into very chilly nights. Fifteen minutes into our return journey, our path disappeared and the terrain looked completely different and almost unrecognizable. The rocky overhangs and small caves seemed to multiply the more we looked for ours.

Anxiety enveloped me as I realized that I had left our map back in the cave. With absolutely no idea what direction to go in, our idyllic and relaxing day was quickly turning to crap. The sun had already slipped below the mountains and it was getting darker—double crap! We had no map, compass, food or filtered water. We didn't even have our headlamps.

Rule #1 is to stay calm. I may have appeared so on the outside, but inside was another story. *What direction do we even go in?* I thought to myself. I knew the cave was relatively close, but that didn't help since I didn't know how to get there. *What in the f*** are we going to do?*

Earlier in the day we had been super careful not to twist an ankle in our Tevas as we cautiously watched each step. Now we scurried through the brush in our sandals, frantically looking for something familiar. I started to visualize a long, cold night embracing each other for warmth under a rocky overhang. Despite anxiety bursting out at the seams, somehow we both managed to keep our cool. The sun continued to set at a rapid pace. We made a decision not to wander off piste as it could lead us nowhere. We found a path heading west and took it, believing it would lead us toward base camp, five and a half hours away. At least that was somewhere. As we reached the top of a hill, we looked down and saw the familiar sight of the river. Could it be? We were back on track! We hugged in a celebration of relief as the Red Wall Cave eventually came into sight. Upon reaching our little home, we collapsed. The adrenaline overdose brought on by our near catastrophe had drained us mentally and physically.

We had come close to being toast. Unfortunately, retirement these days seems to be headed in the same direction for so many for exactly the same reason we got in trouble. When it comes to finances, just as it should in the wilderness, it all starts with a plan.

Talking to the skeleton of a rodent inside Red Wall Cave where I set up camp for the night

I was usually darn good at that. Heck, I was usually great at that. Not only had my driveway business plan worked better than I could have imagined, diligent planning had basically saved my life in the Australian Outback. In *Failure Is Not an Option*, I share the fear-provoking details of driving a 1972 Holden Kingswood station wagon through the interior of Australia where we were warned that we must be prepared for anything and be completely self-sufficient. Little did I know at the time that anything that could go wrong did and that we would use half of our emergency provisions during the first three days of our Outback sojourn. But at least we had them. When you're out in the middle of nowhere, failure is not an option.

You would think that those experiences would have cemented the importance of thorough and prudent planning in my brain. As my Chimanimani story clearly shows, you'd be wrong. I should have known better. The fact is, we set out without a plan and nearly got screwed. Yes, it is rough in the deserts of Australia and Zimbabwe. It is also rough out there in the financial world.

Had I had a plan in Zimbabwe, at a very minimum it would have included trail markers, a map, a headlamp and maybe even a jacket. Similarly, a financial plan should include markers to point you in the right direction, such as an easy-to-follow blueprint that shows where you are in comparison to where you need to be, as well as a light to illuminate your way to financial strength. And since the financial climate fluctuates just like the weather, you need to know how to protect yourself when colder temps set in.

IF IT IS TO BE, IT'S UP TO ME

Many people take the path of least resistance and live their lives by default rather than by design. Financial freedom and living the life you have always imagined aren't just going to happen to you.

A Chinese proverb states:

> *The best time to plant a tree is 20 years ago. The second-best time is now.*

I know that retirement planning isn't the first thing on anyone's mind; however, it's important to get started. If you dawdle, as so many people do, and keep telling yourself *it can wait till later,* you'll wake up one day when you're 55 and find yourself scrambling to figure out how you're going to live in your retirement years.

I've heard people say that they are too young to start worrying about their financial futures, as retirement seems very far off. I agree that they shouldn't agonize about it. Still, the fact is that it is never too soon to begin planning, and if you do get started now, in all probability you will not have to worry down the line. General George Patton said it best:

> *A good plan implemented today is better than a perfect plan implemented tomorrow.*

I know the concept of financial planning can be daunting. Yet the creation of a plan that you understand and know how to implement is one of the most important things you can do at this stage of your life. So let's look at what your financial plan should include and how you can get started.

Like any overseas journey, your road trip to financial success depends on where you're starting from as well as the destination you look forward to reaching. Here are some practical suggestions as you dive into retirement planning on how to get where you're going and how to best avoid getting lost or running into green morays along the way.

KNOW WHERE YOU'RE STARTING FROM

Your specific journey to financial success needs to begin with a detailed map. The photo for the cover of this book was taken inside the 8,000-foot Broken Top peak not far from my home in Bend. If you have never been and your goal is to experience the amazing wildflowers inside this magnificent crater along Soda Creek, you will need to research when the flowers will bloom as well as know your starting point before you can determine what road and trail will get you there. For example, even if you have a single destination in mind, you'll need a very different set of directions if you're leaving from Seattle than if you're leaving from San Francisco. Similarly, to assess your current financial situation, you'll first have to have a clear picture of where your finances are today.

Where are you starting from? Start by calculating your net worth. What are your total assets? This includes everything from the money in your checking or savings accounts—along with any investment accounts in your name—to the equity in your car or the house you may own.

Next, add up your liabilities, including how much you still owe on your car and home, along with any other outstanding debts, including unpaid bills, credit cards, student loans and personal loans.

Then take your assets and subtract your liabilities and there you have it: your net worth. (Assets − Liabilities = Net Worth)

MAKE A BUDGET

A.A. Latimer once said:

> A budget is a mathematical confirmation of your suspicions.

Oh, I know how awful the word *budget* sounds. Please do not put down the book or think of a budget as something negative. Instead, think of budgeting as a roadmap that leads you to your financial future. Creating a budget is not difficult. Today there are plenty of tools to help you get started, including free online tools like Mint, You Need a Budget (YNAB) and GnuCash that can help you come up with—and stick to—a budget. As far as I'm concerned, Mint is the current gold standard for budgeting apps, as it automatically updates and categorizes transactions, creating a picture of spending in real time. You can create your own categories, split ATM transactions into purchases made with that cash, and set budgets that will alert you as you approach your spending death zone. The free service also comes with a complimentary credit score.

This kind of budgeting will help you track every expense you have over the course of a month and separate them into categories such as living expenses, entertainment and, if you're like me, travel. Of course, you'll want to compare the total of these expenses to your monthly, after-tax income. This is where you will immediately determine if you have a surplus with extra funds at the end of the month or a deficit where you owe more than you are bringing in.

Clearly, you want to have a surplus rather than the alternative. Every study I have tracked on millennials indicates that a majority live paycheck to paycheck. They feel debt is their primary issue. We'll address debt in a little bit. Please note that I have not said you need to cut expenses at this point. For now, simply identify where you are currently spending your hard-earned money. You can make the decision to decrease your expenses later in your planning if you determine you should do so.

The time you invest in creating and following a budget will benefit you significantly. I find that many millennials recognize that setting financial goals is important, but they're grasping for ways to reach those goals because they just don't have a plan in place. Maybe that's because their goals aren't as concrete as they may think.

SET AND CLARIFY YOUR GOALS

Being clear about your financial goals can give budgeting a whole new spin. But before you clarify, I say quantify! This is the time to think big because when you think big, believe big and act big, your results will be big. Do you want to own that second home in the mountains one day? For that matter, do you want to own your first home so you can have a dog, paint the walls whatever color you want and have a place that you can truly call your own no matter how big or small?

Tony Robbins says:

> Setting goals is the first step in turning the invisible into the visible.

What do you want to make a reality in your life?

I began writing down my goals in college after listening to Zig Ziglar's audio program titled *Goals: Setting and Achieving Them on Schedule*. He shared an often-quoted study undertaken by Harvard University in 1979 where graduates were asked if they had written goals with action plans for their achievement. Out of the entire graduating class:

- ✓ 3 percent had clearly defined written goals.
- ✓ 12 percent had unwritten goals.
- ✓ 84 percent had no goals in any shape or form.

Ten years later the researchers interviewed the same students who had graduated the prior decade and determined that the 3 percent who had written down their personal goals were 10 times more successful than the 97 percent who had not.

Regardless of your background, education or current skills, the power of personal goal-setting is evident. The same holds true for setting financial goals.

When it comes to your financial goals, the first step is to define them. Assign an estimated cost to each one and be specific. Rather than say, "I want to be wealthy," I suggest saying something more like, "I will have $500,000 in my retirement account at the age of 45" or "I will own my house outright in 15 years." Set goals that are attainable given your expected income, but don't make them too readily attainable. Michael Phelps, the most decorated athlete in Olympic history, said:

> I think goals should never be easy. They should force you to work, even if they are uncomfortable at the time.

Next, it's time to prioritize your financial goals. For example, if you buy that new Jeep Renegade now, will you have enough savings later to buy your first house or travel to Angkor Wat? Which of these goals is most important to you?

A financial plan allows you to set priorities as well as goals, and keep them in front of you. It keeps your finances on track and helps you achieve those goals as soon as possible. You'll want to visit these goals often and update them as needed once you've outlined them.

SAVE MONEY TO REACH YOUR GOALS

Once you decide on the specifics of your goals—which could include life events such as getting married and having a baby—it's time to strategize how to save money to achieve those objectives. You will find it easier to save when you know what you're saving for. Remember, how much money you earn isn't as important as how much money you keep. Once your budget is completed and you know where your money is being allocated each month, it's time to pay yourself first, a concept I previously mentioned. We always seem to pay our essential expenses first. This includes rent or mortgage payments, car payments, utilities, etc. Now it's time to include you in the mix. This is where you systematically deduct a specific amount from each paycheck or from your checking account to fund your new retirement account. If your employer offers a retirement plan, such as a 401(k) or 403(b), jump in immediately. It's that easy. The sooner you start saving, the better off your financial future will be. You will learn firsthand the power of compounding and the excitement of watching your net worth grow and multiply. I look forward to hearing about your successes!

Keep in mind that, as New Jersey Nets player Mike Newlin says:

Genius is perseverance in disguise.

It all starts with having a plan. At the same time, as I discovered during my travels, it is imperative to craft a well-defined route and consider the unique landscapes when in the Australian Outback or in the mountains of Zimbabwe. The key ingredient is having the right person to help you create a plan in the first place.

CHAPTER 9

CHOOSING THE RIGHT GUY

*Unsuccessful people make decisions based on
their current situation; successful people make decisions
based on where they want to be.*

I was starting to look grubby. Really grubby. After five months of traveling down the massive continent of Africa it was time to look human again. I visited a barbershop in Harare to have my lumberjack beard trimmed into a manicured goatee and my curly hair cut and tamed. Oh, how I remember the days of having a thick head of hair. They even trimmed my eyebrows, all for $70 Zimbabwean, the equivalent of $9USD. Next on my short list was the Hutton & Sly department store where I purchased a set of clean, fresh threads. I was a new man and felt like a million bucks. Next stop: one of the seven natural wonders of the world.

Five years earlier, I had graduated college in Rochester, New York. Due to its relatively close proximity to Niagara Falls, weekend road trips found us students visiting the landmark that straddles the international border between Canada and the United States. I thought Niagara had to be the largest and most majestic spill in the universe. That was until I set my eyes on Victoria Falls, roughly twice the height and well over twice the width, resulting in the largest and what must be the most awe-inspiring waterfall on the planet. The Zambezi River is well over a mile wide where it cascades over the basalt lip and plunges more than 350 feet below, forming the natural border of Zimbabwe and Zambia in Africa.

Cooling off to the awe-inspiring Victoria Falls in Zimbabwe, Africa

The moon was one enormous torch illuminating the entire chasm. The atmosphere was soothing and serene, yet eerie. It was the perfect first night at this world heritage site, with the falls generating mists that could be spotted miles away.

Have you ever had a peak experience where you were so in the present moment that you thought to yourself, *This is one of the happiest instances in my life?* I started to remember other magical wonders from my past where I slowed down in the middle of the experience to be grateful in that very moment, including riding a motorcycle on Ios in Greece and horseback riding on the beaches of Montezuma in Costa Rica. Then I brought myself back to the present. I knew I needed to appreciate this particular night, during which I would wind up witnessing an elusive moonbow for the first and only time in my life. I had never even heard of such a planetary extravaganza. Also known as a lunar or white rainbow, a moonbow is produced by light reflected off the surface of the moon (as opposed to direct sunlight) refracting off the moisture created by the mist of the falls. As the light is usually too dim to affect the color receptors in human eyes, it is challenging to distinguish colors in a moonbow. Accordingly, the magnificent moonbow I saw was shimmering white.

When I returned to my campsite, I immediately took out my watercolors and began to paint in my journal a record of nature's show. I later learned that California's Yosemite National Park, Kentucky's Cumberland Falls, Croatia's Plitvice Lakes and, of course, Victoria Falls are a small number of locations around the world known for such moonbows.

My watercolor painting in my journal of the moonbow over Victoria Falls

The next day spelled adventure for my new travel companions and me. We met at the campground located not far from the bustling town of Livingston, which was inundated with international tourists. Operators in the area offer everything from white water rafting and bungee jumping to helicopter and ultralight flights over the falls. The ultralight experience was calling our names, as it would offer aerial views of the falls and an adrenaline rush to boot.

I know what you must be thinking. Yes, this is another ultralight story. However, this one not only took place 20 years earlier than my last ultralight story, it would prove to be a disconcertingly different experience.

We had booked an early evening flight with Batoka Sky, so we arrived at a barren airstrip of cleared scrub brush located just down the road from the campsite at 6:15 p.m. and drew straws to determine who would be the first to soar over the falls. I picked the shortest one, which meant mine would be the very last flight of the day.

An unexpected and hair-raising evening flight over Victoria Falls

The sky was now a deep orange, pink and purple, and the sun was setting at an alarming rate. When I asked Rod, the jovial, rotund pilot, if there would be enough light for my flight, I received a hesitant, "I don't see why not." My gut told me something else. I've learned to listen to that inner voice over lots of years. Somehow it always seems to be right and when I haven't paid attention in the past, I have often paid a price.

My new friend Brad's flight ended with some impressive aerial acrobatics and a helmet was placed on my head. My thoughts spun everywhere: *Is it too dark for one last flight? Are Rod and his crew jeopardizing my life for the $55 price of admission? Oh, what the heck. I'm going for it!*

As I was strapped into the confining passenger seat located directly behind Rod, I did my best to control my apprehension. A high-pitched sputter began when the ground crewman spun the prop of the small engine. After a very short sprint down the makeshift runway of uneven pasture, Rod pulled back on the bar and we were airborne on a steep trajectory. The sun was well below the horizon, yet the deep orange glow reflected off the placid Zambezi River. To the east, the sky was already dark with no sign of the moon. Rod quickly informed me that our flight was currently illegal since it was after dark. I could just make out the falls from above, even though we did not have the light to fly directly over them. My disappointment abruptly turned into anxiety and then sheer fright as my overconfident pilot tried to salvage my experience by attempting some stunts. He quickly accelerated while I rechecked my belts. After revving the engine to capacity, he released the throttle and we veered into a nosedive toward the now-black jungle below. Silence overcame me as I tried to catch my stomach.

Up, up and away ... my sunset ultralight flight over Victoria Falls

"Are you all right back there?" he asked.

I think so, I thought to myself. After another few maneuvers, even he knew it was time to return. *But return where?* The runway was now impossible to see. Before long his crew—and I use that term loosely—figured out that we needed guidance to land. Each went for their aged Toyota Hilux pickup trucks and parked with their headlights illuminating both ends of the runway.

Is this really happening or is this a dream? I wondered, trying to stay calm.

We descended at a nice clip, whizzing just over the roof of the first pickup, and landed smoothly on the grass field. Wow! Another experience for the memory bank.

WHO YOU GONNA CALL?

I guess I don't need to tell you at this point, if you decide to give ultralights a try choose a guy less like Rod and more like Fred, my friend and pilot from Bend. Because when you're flying in the sky with an engine behind you and a hang glider atop, failure is simply not an option.

Let's assume African Rod or Oregon Fred were financial planners. Which one would you want? The seat-of-the-pants guy or the thorough and methodical guy?

Fred shared stories of how challenging it was to learn how to fly his ultralight. "My instructor sat behind me for more than 300 landings before he was completely sure I would land safely every time," he told me. "There is no margin for error. Now I feel safe to take anyone along for a ride."

Just as that instructor made a significant difference when it came to Fred learning to fly, obtaining professional investment guidance can dramatically impact your financial future and keep you from making common, costly mistakes. Even if you feel that you don't need a financial advisor's help at this stage of your life, don't be too quick to write off the value of hiring a professional to assist you.

Here are some reasons to consider working with a planner:

✓   A lack of time in your very busy life, the same reason you might hire someone to mow your lawn or clean your home. Today's world is fast paced and most of us don't have enough hours in the day to get 'er done. Leveraging your time can pay great dividends.

✓   You shy away from numbers and your hair stands up at the thought of mathematical calculations.

✓   Creating a financial roadmap can be difficult. Sometimes you're just too close to your own state of affairs to be objective. You may have unrealistic goals and ignore areas of concern such as debt and out-of-control spending habits. Even if you're like me and actually enjoy learning about money and investing on your own, consider using a planner for an objective second opinion.

✓   Good planners can help you prioritize your goals. Sometimes just making a few key changes can transform everything.

✓ The only thing constant in life is change. Very few plans survive their collision with reality. They need to be updated over time as inevitable changes occur. A professional guide can help keep you on course and heading in the right direction.

✓ Navigating and determining which financial strategies make sense for you in the marketplace is often an absolute nightmare. It seems as though there are endless options to choose from. Talk about information overload! A good planner does the necessary research to match your needs to the best available strategies, products and companies. This can save you from paralysis by analysis.

✓ Advisors can keep you from making bad decisions based on emotions or insufficient information.

✓ Getting a little financial advice can save your relationship. Money is the #1 cause of marital turmoil. Although seeing a financial planner for marriage counseling is not recommended, a good one can help find middle ground on financial issues you may be struggling with.

✓ Peace of mind. After all, the entire point of obtaining professional guidance is to help you get your financial house in order and take a significant burden off your shoulders.

YOU DON'T HAVE TO GO IT ALONE

Let's face it. As much as we like to be independent, we all need a little help now and then. Ashton Eaton, the world's greatest athlete and my hometown hero, is the 2012 and 2016 Olympic Gold Medal winner in decathlon, as well as the world record holder in both the decathlon and heptathlon events as of this writing. Eaton shared with me:

Though I've always had the ability to accomplish my athletic feats, I would have never realized them without a coach. Knowledgeable through experience, a seasoned observer and a technical specialist, a coach provides that critical perspective that one combines with their abilities and turns into accomplishment.

If the world's best athlete needs a coach, don't you think you could benefit from a financial coach?

Since it's critical to choose the right person to help you plan your financial future, you'll want to consider these factors when hiring a financial advisor:

💰 Independent financial advisors offer important advantages. Unlike an in-house advisor, who is limited to the menu of products approved by his employer, independent financial advisors can help investors make informed and objective investment choices from a wide range of financial products. An independent advisor has a single fiduciary responsibility. He is beholden only to you rather than to an investment or insurance company. Historically, various broker-age firms have manufactured products and incentiv-ized their sales force to sell those specific products. Independent advisors have no ties to Wall Street firms and yet they can offer virtually all the top-rat-ed financial investments available today at the same or similar price you'd pay elsewhere.

💰 Personal referrals. Word of mouth is how successful financial planners continue to build their practices. Ask people you respect who they use and why.

THE LOWDOWN ON FINANCIAL ADVISORS

There are three ways that financial planners get compen-sated:

1. Earning commissions generated by the sale of financial products.
2. Charging a percentage of the assets they man-age for you.
3. Charging an hourly rate for objective advice.

Commission-based planners aren't really planners or advi-sors as much as they are salespeople. Many stockbrokers and life insurance agents call themselves financial consultants or representatives. This is like car salesmen calling them-selves transportation consultants. As consumers, we love to buy, but most people have a strong aversion to being sold. I enjoy buying a new car, but the thought of entering a show-room and having a salesman try and sell me a car is down-right uncomfortable.

I have heard stories of clients who pondered why the stellar service they initially received from their commissioned financial advisors dwindled to the point where it became a challenge to get their advisor to even return a phone call. That's because commissioned financial advisors receive a large payout up front when they take over your account, but little income thereafter.

I believe that no matter what field of endeavor one has chosen, compensation tends to breed behavior. It is in everyone's best interest when an advisor has to continually earn his or her client's business. By charging an annual fee, billed quarterly based on the assets the advisor manages, both parties are on the same side of the fence. They want the accounts to increase appropriately over time. When the markets increase, advisors charge the same percentage as they do when the markets decline, which they inevitably will in certain years. So it's in the advisors' interest to help ensure that their clients' accounts do not drop excessively and, instead, continue to grow over time.

In my experience, preeminent advisors do everything possible to ensure that their goals align with their clients', removing as much of the sales process as possible from the equation. These financial advisors:

💰 Charge for their expertise. How much do you think most financial advisors charge for their advice? The answer is nothing! Can you imagine this being the case with your attorney or CPA? Many financial advisors only get compensated when they sell you an investment or insurance product. Is this in your best interest? Of course not. Successful individuals who take their finances seriously prefer to pay for advice rather than be sold financial products that may not be the best fit for them.

💰 Guarantee your satisfaction. Once the financial planning process is complete, they refund 100 percent of the planning fee if their clients do not feel that their expectations regarding the value they got out of the plan have been met or surpassed.

💰 Have access to the vast majority of A+ rated investment and insurance companies from around the globe. And since they do not represent a specific investment or insurance company, their only responsibility is to *you*.

💰 Share how they are compensated without having to be asked.

It is important to do your due diligence, as bad and biased advice is out there. I see the consequences of such advice on a regular basis. On the other hand, most of the advisors I know and have met are good, honest people who have decided to get into this line of work for the right reasons.

Part of choosing the right advisor is finding someone who specializes in exactly what you need at the stage you are at in your financial life. Any journey—financial or otherwise—can be risky. If you're a seasoned traveler, through having the right tools and detailed planning, you can mitigate those risks. The last thing you want is to invite those risks that could be avoided. I figured this out on Bolivia's Death Road.

CHAPTER 10

LIFE-AND-DEATH DECISIONS

Life is about choices. Some we regret.
Some we're proud of. Some will haunt us forever.
We are what we choose to be.
—Graham Brown

The first glimpse of La Paz will, literally, take your breath away. At an elevation of almost 12,000 feet above sea level, it's the world's highest capital city. An estimated 800,000 Bolivians live inside the bowl-like depression that resembles the caldera of an enormous volcano and is surrounded by the snow-capped Andes reaching heights greater than 18,000 feet.

My blood felt thin with the mountain temperatures. I gasped for oxygen that seemed mostly absent as I wandered the colorful markets and alleys in search of a cozy café.

Downtown has a vibrant cultural energy with historical museums, cathedrals and colonial palaces that ooze character. The steep valley slopes on the city's outskirts are precariously weighed down with ramshackle homes of the city's poorest residents, reminding me of the *favelas* of Rio de Janeiro.

Bolivia, a landlocked country in western South America located about halfway down the continent, is South America's poorest country, with greater than 60 percent of its people living below the national poverty line. Bolivians are also known for having the largest proportion of indigenous people in Latin America. I found them to be kind and unassuming, with tight-knit families of numerous generations often living together under one roof. These pleasant people found a way into my heart.

The country's topography—from high mountains to barren plains to lowland rain forests—is just as memorable as its people. But it wasn't until I traveled to the Amazon Basin, located 260 miles to the north, that I truly acquired a sense of how incredibly wide-ranging the landscape is in this awe-inspiring country. I also didn't have the slightest idea that I was in for the longest, most spine-chilling crossing of my life.

I RISKED MY LIFE ON A BOLIVIAN BUS TO SAVE $60

A Bolivian man warned me not to take the 18-hour bus ride from La Paz to Rurrenabaque. "Flying is much safer," he said. But as a 26-year-old backpacker with four months of the journey left, I was motivated by a propensity for adventure and the desire to save my precious *dinero*. The bus ride would take me on the world's most treacherous thoroughfare: the road that connects the heights of La Paz to the rain forest at sea level, known as the Death Road.

Bolivia's Death Road: The scariest ride of my life!

Every year, an estimated 300 people are killed on Yungas Road as numerous buses plummet into the valley. Luckily—or unluckily, depending on your perspective—I didn't know that at the time. Surrounded by vertical mountain precipices and overhangs, the snaking dirt road had been cut into the side of the Cordillera Oriental Mountains in the 1930s by Paraguayan prisoners. Today it's still one and a half lanes of rutted dirt, gravel and water-filled potholes.

How can this be a one-way thoroughfare? I wondered.

It's not. It's a two-way road.

Terrified does not even begin to describe the panic I felt as the sheer cliff face dropped 1,800 feet into a verdant abyss to my left. No guardrails. No reflectors. No sanity. I felt as if I were riding the X2 rollercoaster at California's Six Flags Magic Mountain without a lap bar restraint.

Where's my climbing harness and rope when I need it? I thought. *What am I doing here?*

I knew I had a sleepless night ahead of me.

With every switchback, I gazed down into the foggy valley and held my breath. If that wasn't scary enough, an archaic lorry filled with an unrecognizable species of vegetables came toward us around one of the innumerable blind bends. Apparently, we drew the short straw: One of the passengers hopped off the bus and began to guide us backward to a slightly wider spot in the road so the truck could squeeze by. Suddenly the people at the back of the bus started shouting, trying to get the driver to stop. Instead, he kept reversing. As fellow passengers became more and more panicked, I heard my new friends—two female backpackers from England— begin to cry in a state of shock and disbelief. I took an enormous breath and told myself, *It's not my time yet.*

I felt like kissing the muddy, red earth and visiting the Our Lady of Candelaria Church in the main square the following morning when our bus finally reached Rurrenabaque, the small town known as the gateway to the rain forests. After the most terrifying 18 hours of my life, I was relieved beyond words not to have become a permanent part of the Bolivian landscape.

The previous afternoon I had left La Paz clad in a heavy sweater and boots to deal with the freezing temps of the Andes. Now the oppressive, hot, humid jungle air asphyxiated me. Yes, it was even worse than seal-coating driveways on hot asphalt during a heat wave back home, but I didn't even care. I had survived the Death Road!

So all these years later I have to ask myself, *What was I thinking? Could I have gotten there in a way that was much safer?*

Of course I could have.

I have heard Ed Viesturs relive moments where he was a few hundred feet from reaching the summit of one of the world's tallest peaks and turned around, as the risk of the snow giving way was too great. He said, "It doesn't matter how good you are—in the mountains, just when you think you're in control, you aren't." I knew that I had no control of the bus as it puttered along the road from hell. I also realized that while I couldn't do anything to change the outcome of whether we would survive, deciding to get on the bus in the first place had been all me.

This is also the name of the game in the financial world, where the objective is to attain our goals with the least amount of risk. It's okay to take risks but—as I experienced on that bus and during night diving on Catalina Island—not stupid ones. One of the most effective ways to lessen your risk is to recognize the risks you're running. So, let's embark on a speed-dating course about risk as it relates to finances. Here are six risks you'll want to be able to identify, since chances are good that you will face them on your financial journey. If you don't account for these risks, life is going to suck—you won't be in for 18 horrendous hours like on my Death Road journey, you'll be looking at 18 years to life.

1. Inflation Risk

One could argue that the greatest threat to financial independence is inflation. Simply put, inflation means that every year your money buys a little—or a lot—less than it did the year before. The average U.S. inflation rate has been just under 3.5 percent. This may not sound like much, especially when we compare it to other countries like Venezuela, which experienced a 475 percent inflation rate in 2016 over 2015. However, even a 3.5 percent rate of inflation means that prices will double every 20 years. In 1980, the year the first millennials were born, the average cost of a new car was $7,574. Today that same car costs $34,000. In 1980, the average new home cost $62,900. Today the average cost of a new home is more than $365,000. Let's look at how this will impact your financial future. If 25-year-olds have a goal to retire on $50,000 a year, by age 45 they will need $100,000 to purchase what $50,000 purchases today. By retirement at age 65, the doubling will have taken place again and $200,000 will be needed to acquire what that $50,000 purchased 40 years earlier. So it's critical to plan for inflation in order to maintain your purchasing power.

2. Millennials Have a Longer Life Expectancy

Advancements in medicine, technology and personal health are allowing us to live longer. During the last century, our life expectancy has almost doubled and just since 1990 it has increased by about six years. It is now estimated that millennials will retire for nearly the same amount of years as they will work. According to the Census Bureau, by 2050 the number of centenarians around the world is expected to grow to 1,000,000. Last year, Hallmark Cards Inc. sold 85,000 100th birthday cards. Praying, eating raw eggs and staying single are the keys to a long life, according to Emma Morano of Pollanza, Italy. She is the oldest person living today and the only person alive who was born in the 1800s, having celebrated her 117th birthday in December of 2016. I believe the trick is growing up without growing old, and replacing rocking chairs with skis, stand-up paddleboards and golf clubs. I fully expect that's how the millennial generation will age. However, longevity means that planning for retirement will take on more importance than ever before.

3. Market Risk

We don't like to think about markets heading south, but as I previously shared, economic recessions have occurred throughout the history of modern economics. We have experienced 10 recessions between 1945 and 2017. The average duration of these recessions is 10 months. Many people have referred to our last economic setback as the Great Recession, since by many measures it was the most severe post-World War II recession we've had. But there's absolutely no reason to think that will be the last one we face.

Now let me ask you a question. If the market loses 50 percent one year and then increases 50 percent the following year, where are you? It's fun for me to ask this question because, without fail, most people will say that you are back where you started. In actual fact, your portfolio has experienced a 25 percent decline. Let's test the math. After $100,000 loses 50 percent of its value, you have $50,000. When $50,000 increases by 50 percent you have $75,000, which means that 25 percent of the portfolio has disappeared. In this scenario, you would need a 100 percent return just to break even and recoup your losses! Once in retirement this can be detrimental. However, during the accumulation phase that you're currently in, when the market retreats you end up purchasing more shares with each and every dollar. With appropriate asset allocation and diversification—two topics we have already discussed—you help decrease the downside risk. If your portfolio loses 10 percent instead of 50 percent, you will only need an 11 percent return to break even. A far better circumstance.

4. Social Insecurity

Not too long ago, people retired at the age of 65 and received a gold watch after spending an entire career working for the same company. They had a reasonable expectation that they could live out the rest of their lives comfortably, thanks to their company pension, Social Security and a steady flow of dividends and interest from safe, conservative stocks and bonds. Times have certainly changed!

In the past, Social Security was considered a sure thing. Today I label this program Social *Insecurity*, as its foundation is cracked, and this crack will only grow larger and more dangerous. Nearly 61 million Americans will receive $918 billion in benefits this year. The number of individuals receiving benefits is projected to grow to 91 million in 2035, the same year that the program will likely be insolvent. Why would Social Security run out of money? It all gets back to math again. In 1950, 16.5 people in the work force funded the system for every benefactor. Today, only 2.8 people fund every benefactor. Since 2010, the program has taken in less money than it pays out in benefits, adding to the program's estimated shortfall of $8.6 trillion. If any company were operating on the same basis as the current Social Security program, it would have been put out of business years ago. If you're a millennial, I have some sour advice; don't include Social Security in your financial plan. If the program somehow winds up providing you a supplemental income in retirement, just consider it icing on the cake.

5. Say Farewell to Defined-Benefit Pension Plans

These plans have been phased out, and the shift from traditional, guaranteed pensions to 401(k)s has made retirement a riskier prospect. Before, your employer managed the investments and controlled spending. Now, it's all on you. Retirees were certainly startled in 2008 when they witnessed their holdings inside their retirement accounts plummet. With an estimated 10,000 people retiring a day, it's no wonder that the primary concern among many retirees is simply making ends meet.

6. Not Preparing for the Unexpected (Death and Disability)

You can't predict the future, but you can plan for it. This involves more than just managing your budget and growing your savings. It's very important to protect your assets by having adequate life insurance to ensure your loved ones will be okay financially if you die. The purpose of life insurance is to provide enough money for your family to live on after you pass away. This should include enough to replace a portion of your income, cover debt, children's education and final expenses. More than 40 percent of Americans say they would feel the financial impact within six months if the primary wage earner died. That's not good.

The least expensive way to financially protect your family is through term life insurance. If you die before the policy does, the insurance company pays your heirs a tax-free death benefit. If you live, the company keeps your premium. The average cost of a $250,000 20-year term life policy is $275 a year for a healthy 30-year-old male. That's less than $25 per month. You can't afford not to have such protection.

An interesting statistic is that during the course of your career, you are three and a half times more likely to be injured and need disability coverage than you are to die and need life insurance. One of your most valuable assets may not be the first thing that comes to mind when you think about your finances. It's not your house, car or retirement account: It's your ability to make a living. An unexpected disability could mean the death of your income, a condition that health insurance and Medicare won't cover. Disability insurance helps replace a major portion of your income when you're injured or sick and unable to work. Think of it as paycheck protection as well as a way to protect your home, since a mortgage payment is often your most significant monthly expense. Having disability insurance can provide a sense of security, knowing that should the unexpected arise, you'll still receive a monthly income.

Many would say you are an unlucky generation as you face the six serious risks we've just reviewed. I say it's all about making your own luck in your life. It's about how often we put ourselves into positions where we can be lucky. Luck has less to do with what happens to you and more to do with how you think and act. I have been fortunate to experience a great deal of luck and serendipity over my years of travel to over 65 countries on four continents. This good fortune continued during a recent visit to Cuba before President Obama opened it up to Americans. But I never would have experienced that had I not pushed to make it happen.

CHAPTER 11

GETTING IT DONE

*I am a great believer in luck, and I find the harder
I work, the more I have of it.*
—Thomas Jefferson

In my first book, *Failure Is Not an Option,* I shared my keenness for experiencing countries before they are open to Americans. I went to Vietnam in 1993, a year before President Clinton lifted a 19-year trade embargo that had been in place since the war. Was I nervous to land in Ho Chi Minh City? Of course I was, but I have always yearned for experiences that would forever have an impact on me.

Like Vietnam, I had been long drawn to the island nation of Cuba, located so close and yet so far from American shores. Hearing stories over the years from my good friend Jeff Monson—who visited Cuba through the back door of Mexico back in 1990, at a time when no one thought Americans would ever be able to travel there legally—only added to my desire.

In April of 2015, my journey there became an idea whose time had arrived.

Cuba, here I come! Even if I had to be shrewd, like Jeff, and enter via Mexico.

Make that *here* **WE** *come.* My most important goal had been to share a true third-world experience with my two children, Sophie and Jack. Just as this type of travel had done for me, I was confident this would help them better appreciate the lifestyle they have back at home in Bend. So I decided to take them with me. My other goal was to beat McDonald's, Starbucks, Carnival cruise ships and the influx of predatory capitalism and American tourists that I knew would appear in masses once the U.S. economic ban was lifted. Cuba is a country with unlimited possibilities and I hope it won't sell its soul as it grows up. But I wasn't confident about how well it would withstand the onslaught. Who would have known that within a year after our journey, President Obama would lift the economic embargo that had been in place since 1959 and become the first U.S. president to visit Cuba in nearly 90 years? Sometimes timing is everything.

Our two-week journey started in the capital of Havana and took us around the western half of the country. No tours or hotels for us! Our Renault rental car was relatively new, and so didn't encompass the marvelous character of the thousands of vintage American cars that still remain scattered throughout the country. On the other hand, it didn't break down, either.

Sophie and Jack playing with a boy in Havana, Cuba

We stayed in a *casa particular* each night—the home of a Cuban family that rents rooms out to travelers. This was a fun and effective way to learn more about local customs and culture. The bedsprings spoke at full volume to our backs and most toilets did not have seats. Still, their homes were always immaculate and exuded a warmth that welcomed us with open arms.

"MODERN" CUBA

I quickly realized that it felt as if Cuba had gone to sleep in the late 1800s and never really awakened. The capital city of Havana has a flavor all its own with an unmistakable aroma of tropical fruit, tobacco leaves and rum mixed with fumes from belching buses, rotten garbage and broken sewer pipes. This historical city is enchanting and yet disheartening as decades of neglect, grime and humidity have led to mildewed walls of chipped cement and collapsing balconies. These once magnificent buildings now face irrevocable decay. Just strolling down the undulating cobblestone streets required caution. The relics of colonial-era buildings resemble Madrid, yet the destruction reminded me of Karachi. It was hard to fathom that the lavish American Riviera and art deco playground of South Beach, Miami, lay just 225 miles to the north.

Despite the crumbling buildings and debris-strewn streets, I found Cuba to be intoxicating—and I am not even alluding to their famous Havana rum, which is less expensive than bottled water. Locals and visitors alike enjoy sipping their famed Mojitos, Daiquiris and Cuba Libres. Music is everywhere, quite literally on the streets and in most bars and restaurants. Jazz, Cuban hip-hop and of course salsa keep Cuba's beat. Sexy cabarets rival those in Las Vegas and Rio de Janeiro. No wonder Ernest Hemingway's favorite place on earth was his home in the outskirts of Havana.

AN ATTITUDE OF GRATITUDE

Cuba is a country that can frustrate you one minute and inspire you the next. Still, my children fell in love with Cuba. Our journey there opened their eyes wide and made them realize how very fortunate they are to have been born and raised in beautiful Bend, Oregon. They returned home with a new appreciation for pretty much everything around them. They embraced their beds that didn't have springs poking through the mattress, hot showers, toilets with seats, tidy streets that weren't deteriorated and supermarkets filled with unlimited supplies of food. They began to focus on what they were grateful for, which was great to witness, as I'm a firm believer in *what you focus on expands*. If we can learn to be more grateful for the good we already have, more of that goodness will enter our lives. Unfortunately, the same can be said if we center our attention on what we lack. Would you rather have a wealth consciousness or a poverty consciousness?

David, Jack and Sophie Rosell, Havana, Cuba

While I suggest visiting Cuba soon, as much of its charm will change fast once other influences establish themselves on the island, traveling there is not a necessity to appreciate what you already have in your life, right here at home.

Perhaps you're already living life with this kind of appreciation. In fact, the Cuban people, who aren't grabby and greedy, remind me of the millennial generation, who also seem to choose a wealth of experiences over wealth in their bank accounts. Millennials spend more time and money on everything from social events and concerts to athletic pursuits and cultural experiences. Happiness seems to trump career status and possessions. Rather than purchase new cars and flat screen TVs, they're rocking out at Coachella, hiking the Inca Trail, backcountry skiing or helping to improve our world and the people in it. Living a happy, meaningful life of purpose is about creating, sharing and capturing memories and opportunities. Money can buy a house but not a home. It can buy a bed but not sleep. It can buy a clock but not time.

Money is such a fascinating topic. If you were to talk to 10 different people, each would probably have a different relationship and past experiences with it. I believe few people have made friends with money. Instead, many have a regrettably contentious relationship with it. They hoard it. Or they worship it. Or they fear it, afraid they will not have enough or afraid it will not provide what they need.

At the end of the day, I believe we all basically want the same things in life—to be happy, healthy, to be financially secure and to have good relationships with family and friends. That's true wealth.

RICH VERSUS WEALTHY: OUR RELATIONSHIP TO MONEY

Cubans have faced extreme hardships over the past half a century, while the Castros and their high-echelon government cronies have lived high on the hog. Even so, the country's inhabitants are wealthy in numerous ways.

Wealthy? you may be asking yourself.

Yes, wealthy.

In Cuba, it's not all about money. There's a strong emphasis on relationships and living life fully rather than indulgently.

Imagine if I shared stories of the markets in the United States piled with food flown in from around the world, stories of doctors who give out pills to stop adults from eating and our children from being so energetic at school, kids leaving school with depression, high suicide rates, deaths from drug overdoses and a population that doesn't even know their next-door neighbors. In Cuba, you'd be hard pressed to ever see a gun or drugs. One can walk the city streets late at night and not worry about being robbed or mugged.

They might consider us rich, but by comparison they would realize that they're wealthier than we are when it comes to daily living.

While many millennials have an association with money that leans more to the Cuban perspective that money is just a medium of exchange, many don't really understand how it works, grows or compounds. I hope this book has helped on that front. But that's not enough. We can shift the paradigm by asking ourselves, *Is having money and being wealthy the same thing?*

Once again, we just have to look to Cuba for the answer.

Before the revolution, Havana was one of the world's most advanced cities. Today, it's extremely poor and decayed. In many ways, Cubans seem like first-world people trapped in a third-world country. Most people live in diminutive houses and own very few possessions. In a country where the monthly salary for a doctor is the equivalent of $25USD, few families own cars and they certainly don't have iPads or IRAs.

I imagined the Cuban people would have felt like everything was falling apart faster than they could pick up the pieces, and yet they somehow have a spirit, a love of life and a hope that is infectious. I thought to myself, *They have so little. We have so much back in the United States and yet they seem significantly happier. How could this be? Why is this?*

Could it be the weather? I wondered. Odds are that the percentage of happy people is higher than in our weather-challenged areas like Alaska or North Dakota because of this simple reason, but many places have beautiful weather and people who aren't as joyful.

Cuba is a poor country, but rich in culture and heritage. Could that be it? Yes, Cubans are a wonderful example of how art improves the quality of life. I'm confident that the cigars and rum also help. But there must be something more that keeps them happy.

Maybe it's their cultural traditions? Cubans and music are inseparable. Everywhere you go, a lively rhythm fills the air. Cubans have music and dance in their blood. But in the end, I believe they're happier because they are grateful for what it is they already have, they value true relationships, and they are hopeful for the future even when things may seem rather bleak at times.

HOPE

The verb to hope is defined as *to desire with expectation of obtainment, to expect with confidence.* As John Maxwell stated:

> *Where there is no hope in the future, there is no power in the present.*

That's a message we would do well to pay attention to. Unfortunately, I have noticed a lot of people are currently lacking hope for a brighter future. This is clearly not the easiest of times for many of you millennials who are just fed up, feeling hopeless about your own financial situation, about our government and about a life's journey you may feel is arduous. But you're sure not alone. Many people are fearful, confused and anxious, feelings that were accentuated following a presidential election that split our country in half.

Whenever confronted with hardships, whether they involve money, relationships or politics, we can choose to either numb ourselves and paddle down da Nile (otherwise known as *denial*) or take action and paddle upstream on the Deschutes River (or wherever) to conquer whatever challenges we face. On the financial front, for example, we can wave the white flag and give up on any possibility for a post-working life of freedom or folly, or we can start saving for that future even though it means some uncomfortable belt-tightening now. As I've said repeatedly, the tougher you are on yourself today, the easier life will be on you later.

Whether you live in Cuba, Africa, South America or here in the States, life is not straightforward and trouble-free. But things, most often, have a way of working out. They just do. We've made it through continual financial downturns including the Great Depression and most recently the Great Recession, among others in between. We've also made it through the never-ending changes in government parties and policies. Shall we count all the wars we've fought? The list of challenges goes on and on. In the end, it's important to recognize that difficult times often bring out the best in us as it enables us to develop resiliency.

Even during what seems to be a dark time in our country, it's imperative to remember that winter always precedes spring. As I look out the window from my home here in Bend, snow continues to pile up at alarming and record-breaking rates. Roofs are caving in—including on the elementary school down the street from my home. My kids were out of school for nine days because all the schools had to be checked for safety. But the schools would have likely closed anyway, since many of the roads are impassable. People are either stuck at home or climbing onto their frozen roofs to try and prevent the water from pouring in because of ice dams.

During all this chaos, it is important to appreciate the fact that the snow insulates the ground so that things will grow and bloom in the spring. Maybe that's what's happening in general with our country right now as well as with your generation in particular.

James Baldwin said:

> Not everything that is faced can be changed. But nothing can be changed until it is faced.

This is where we're at. The spring is not here yet, but it will come. We just need to make sure to face our challenges and do the right thing on all fronts until then.

LOOKING TO THE FUTURE

If you're not confused, you're not paying attention.
—Tom Peters

We've covered a lot of ground around the globe together, visiting attention-grabbing places such as Nepal, Chile, Kenya, Malawi, Catalina, Zimbabwe, Bolivia and Cuba. We've also covered a significant amount of financial ground, learning essential concepts that will help direct your financial future. Let's review:

💰 Every climb, no matter how big or small, starts with a single step. In the world of finance, it starts with some core basics, such as compound interest. **You have to pay yourself first**.

💰 In order to have money work for you instead of you working for money, you must **delay gratification**.

💰 **Get the right tools.** Learn about the different financial homes (investment accounts—IRAs 401(k)s, Roth IRAs, etc.) and the furniture to place inside of your accounts (investment vehicles—stocks, mutual funds and ETFs).

💰 **Diversify,** both in terms of owning a combination of the major asset classes as well as tax classifications so that more money ends up in your pocket and less in Uncle Sam's.

💰 **Play it smart.** Don't chase returns, time the markets or hold on to too much of your own company's stock.

💰 **Get started sooner rather than later.** As Zig Ziglar put it so eloquently:

If you can't take a huge step to begin with, take as big a step as you can but take it now!

💰 Create a well-crafted **plan** and find the right person to help guide you.

💰 **Overcome the six risks** every millennial faces: inflation risk, longevity risk, market risk, Social Insecurity, the end of pension plans and the possibility of disability.

💰 Shift the way you think and review your priorities; **have an attitude of gratitude** and hope for our future.

If only money could talk. Wouldn't it be interesting to ask it direct questions, such as, *How would you like to be used?* or *What good can you do in the world?* or *What is your purpose?* Since money doesn't have a voice, it occurs to me that we don't just need to learn more about it, we need to make friends with it as well.

Even if making money isn't your be-all and end-all, that doesn't mean that you shouldn't treat money with the respect it deserves. Years ago, I learned that creating a welcoming space that honors the money you already have is a way to attract more money into your life. Since then, I have organized the bills in my wallet so they face the same direction and are in order from the ones to 20s and so on. I suggest you give this simple tactic a try, since I believe the more we become aware of how to respectfully handle money, the more we open the door for more of it to enter our lives.

The bottom line? We're looking to create a helpful connection with money. Have you ever asked yourself what your own relationship with money is all about? I've heard some people say money is evil. I couldn't disagree more. Dave Ramsey believes that:

> *Money is not good or evil. It has no morals or intentions on its own. Money reflects the character of the user.*

Alan Cohen takes that a step further, stating:

> Money is not the root of all evil ... ignorance is the root
> of all evil. People do cruel and foolish things for money
> because they feel oppressed by a sense of lack. If people
> knew their power to generate wealth, they would never
> fight or hurt each other over money.

You probably know someone who buys things they don't need with money they don't have while trying to impress people they don't even like. Can you imagine trying to explain that to a Cuban? That's not a positive relationship with money!

Through my years of travel, I have learned a great deal about different cultures and customs around the world. I have learned to appreciate and welcome the differences in people rather than condemn and criticize.

Most importantly, I have learned a lot more about myself, which I have come to realize is a never-ending journey. My priorities in life have certainly shifted over time, but I remain a proponent of emphasizing quality of life first. By doing so, we enhance our standard of living.

Your career is what you're paid for and your calling is what you're made for. What is your calling or purpose over this 90-year dream we call life? Money will fund a purpose, but it won't provide one. I think we often complicate things when it's really quite simple. Find what makes you happy. Follow your bliss and you'll never look back.

My wish for you is that you succeed beyond your wildest imagination and live the life you have always imagined. That you play as hard as you work. And that you never, ever stop dreaming. Most of all, I wish you happiness. But it's up to you to make that happen!

Jim Rohn said:

> *If you really want to do something, you'll find a way. If you don't, you'll find an excuse.*

Ski-film pioneer Warren Miller, who has traveled the globe in search of the wild steep and deep, has always had the uncanny ability to capture the adventure, wonder and beauty that is skiing and that is life. He ends each and every film with the same statement, which impacts me just as strongly today as it did in my youth:

> *If you don't do it this year, you'll be one year older when you do.*

I believe the best is yet to come. Let's make that happen, starting today.

David Rosell

ABOUT DAVID

David's inspiration and zest for life have been shaped by a lifetime of international travel and adventure. With a current tally of more than 65 countries on four different continents, his quest for extreme travel has included hitchhiking from Nairobi, Kenya to Capetown, South Africa, and climbing the infamous peaks of the Nepalese Himalayas. He was one of the privileged to partake in tearing down the Berlin Wall.

As a recipient of a Retirement Distribution Certificate from the University of Pennsylvania's Wharton School of Business, David excels making complicated financial planning topics easy to understand. He has been featured on CNN Money, MSN Money, Fox Business News, Yahoo Finance and NPR, as well as in *US News & World Report* and the *Chicago Tribune*. His company, Rosell Wealth Management, was a select finalist in 2008 for the management of the $500,000,000 Oregon 529 College Fund.

An accomplished speaker, David has addressed international audiences, including the Million Dollar Roundtable® and Vistage Worldwide. He's the past chairman of the Bend, Oregon, Chamber of Commerce and the City Club of Central Oregon.

His life in Bend is constantly inspired by his two children, Sophie and Jack. When he's not working or parenting, David indulges his passions for downhill skiing, mountain biking, paddleboarding and rock climbing.

For more information about personal finance—including videos,
articles and other resources—go to:

www.RosellWealthManagement.com

David addresses international audiences numbering in the thousands, including the Million Dollar Round Table®.

To inquire about having David speak at your event, please email: speaking@RosellWealthManagement.com

David Rosell in his Bend, Oregon office

If one advances confidently in the direction of his dreams,
and endeavors to live the life which he has imagined,
he will meet with a success unexpected in common hours.
—Henry David Thoreau

Rosell Wealth Management
550 NW Franklin Ave.
Suite 368
Bend, OR 97703